BLACKOUT

HOW THE ELECTRIC INDUSTRY
EXPLOITS AMERICA

Gordon L. Weil

Nation Books
New York

BLACKOUT
How the Electric Industry Exploits America

Published by
Nation Books
An Imprint of Avalon Publishing Group, Inc.
245 West 17th Street, 11th Floor
New York, NY 10011

AVALON
publishing group incorporated

Copyright © Gordon L. Weil 2006

Nation Books is a co-publishing venture of the Nation Institute and Avalon Publishing
Group Incorporated.

Library of Congress Cataloging-in-Publication Data

ISBN-10: 1-56025-812-8
ISBN-13: 978-1-56025-812-4

9 8 7 6 5 4 3 2 1

Book design by Bettina Wilhelm

Printed in the United States of America
Distributed by Publishers Group West

BLACKOUT

Also by Gordon L. Weil

The European Convention on Human Rights
A Handbook on the European Economic Community (editor)
A Foreign Policy for Europe
The Benelux Nations
Trade Policy in the 70's
The Gold War (with Ian Davidson)
The Long Shot: George McGovern Runs for President
The Consumer's Guide to Banks
Election '76
American Trade Policy: A New Round
Sears, Roebuck, U.S.A.
The Welfare Debate of 1978
America Answers a Sneak Attack

For my daughter Anne Weil
and my son Richard Weil and his wife Laura Goldberg
And for my granddaughters, Sadie Anne and Sabine Hannah Weil

CONTENTS

Preface

This book follows twenty-five years of working on matters relating to the electric industry both in government and as a consultant. Much of the book's content and many of its conclusions are based on my experience as chairman of the national committee of state energy agencies, head of the Maine Office of Energy Resources, Maine's first public advocate, and a consultant assisting consumer-owned utilities and large customers or groups of customers. (I must note that I participated only in the earliest stages of Maine's electric industry restructuring and am not responsible in any way for the result, which I find to be the most successful state effort in the United States.)

In the course of my work, I continually learned from my contacts with consumer-owned and investor-owned utilities and their customers. Along with other power purchasing efforts, I represented customers in their relationships with Enron and was fortunate enough to understand its weakness in time to spare my clients undoubted harm. I have participated as an expert witness before regulatory commissions in the United States, including the Federal Energy Regulatory Commission, and in Canada, and have learned from these experiences. I was the chairman of the negotiations on the New England single transmission tariff. I have worked for clients from Washington State to Nova Scotia to Florida and places in between. Many of the matters discussed here stem from my own direct involvement. Because of my role in a range of electric industry matters, I have been contractually required to maintain information confidential at points in this book while telling the story.

Over the past decade, I have encountered a persistent belief that the transformation of this artificially regulated industry into a competitive business was working well and needed only a few more "tweaks" to produce benefit for customers. However, the tweaking has grown more massive and the results more disappointing—at least for the customers.

Two problems have become clear. First, after successful efforts under President Franklin D. Roosevelt's New Deal to prevent the electric industry from being dominated by a handful of powerful, national companies, the failure of the so-called competitive model has led to precisely such domination. Second, customers have never been well protected from the excesses of the companies dominating the industry, and they are probably worse off under the new regime than they were in the "bad" old days of the monopoly model. They are usually exploited without even knowing it. In fact, because the electric business is complicated and customers have always been overcharged, it is difficult for customers to recognize the excess charges they are paying.

My purpose in this book is both to reveal much of what has been hidden from the general public and to suggest how matters may be improved. Much consumer apathy results from ignorance about the electric industry and the sense that consumers have no power to bring about change. Because the voice of the consumer is weak and because of the pernicious effect of campaign contributions by the industry, politicians do not take up the consumer's cause but instead acquiesce in the growing power of the major electric industry companies.

The motto of Columbia University, where I earned a Ph.D., keeps suggesting itself to me: *In lumine tuo videbimus lumen* (In Thy light shall we see light; Psalms 36:9). Perhaps this book will shed some light on the industry founded to give us light.

An organizational note: sidebars at the end of some chapters explain technical terms more fully than in the text itself. These sidebars are meant as a general reference not only for the chapter in which they are found but for the book as a whole. They do not include all relevant industry terms, only those used in the text. They are listed under the relevant chapter titles in the Contents.

ACKNOWLEDGMENTS

S ome of the people with whom I have been privileged to work have contributed to my understanding of the issues discussed here and allowed me to participate in the energy business. I thank them. Maine Governor Joseph E. Brennan gave me the first opportunity to enter what would turn out to be my principal profession. Among my clients, I thank especially John Clark, general manager of the Houlton Water Company, George Stoutamyer, former superintendent and now board member of Madison Electric Works, Paul Fortin, a former Madison board member and formerly responsible for power purchasing at U.S. paper mills owned by SAPPI, Ltd., and Dwight Curley, who taught me much about natural gas, notably when he was president of the Champlain Pipeline project. Greg Williams, an attorney dealing with FERC matters as a staff counsel and in private practice, has been a colleague and friend who managed to get me involved in some of the most interesting matters.

In my own consulting firm, I acknowledge above all the contributions of Kristin S. Roberts, who is dedicated, competent, and capable of prodigious work. I also have learned much from my associates David H. Thorne and Ross McEacharn, who is former director of the New England Power Exchange. Of course, there are many others in the electric business to whom I owe thanks. Richard Weil, C.F.A., provided helpful advice on hedging.

The Power Report, the daily online newsletter of the Power Marketing Association, deserves special mention as an unusually valuable resource.

In writing this book and seeing it through to publication, I greatly appreciate the dedication and counsel of Phyllis Westberg, my agent at Harold Ober Associates, and Carl Bromley, editorial director of Nation Books, who guided me to substantial improvements.

Finally, Roberta M. Weil, my wife, gave me the support and criticism that are essential to such an undertaking, and I remain grateful for her forbearance and help.

Gordon L. Weil
Harpswell, Maine
December 2005

The Bundled Utility

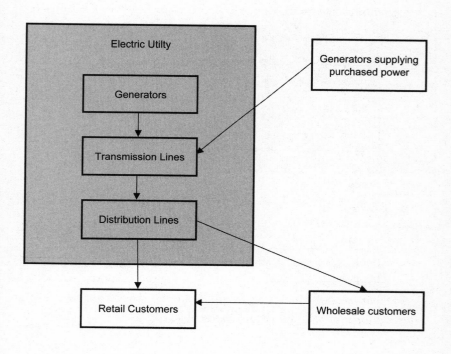

Electric Utilty

Generators

Transmission Lines

Distribution Lines

Generators supplying purchased power

Retail Customers

Wholesale customers

The Unbundled Utility

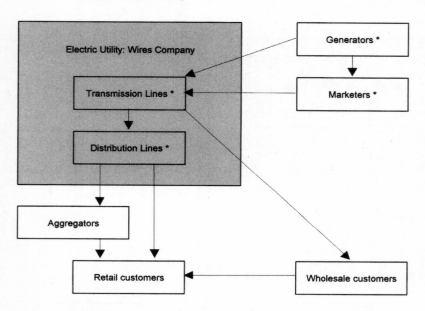

* May be owned by the same company
or by different companies

INTRODUCTION

Augustus 14, 2003, was a pleasant summer Thursday. As the clock passed 4 P.M., people working in their air-conditioned offices in New York and Toronto could begin to think about going home for the evening; probably the last thing they were thinking of was electricity. By 4:30 P.M., they would be thinking of nothing else. Much of the northeastern United States and the Canadian province of Ontario had suddenly lost electric power. Before the electricity returned, millions would either walk home or find themselves stranded for the night. The blackout reminded people of just how dependent they are on distant generators and giant transmission lines—on an industry they barely understand.

Electricity was not invented; it was discovered. One leading scientist who explored its characteristics was Benjamin Franklin. In 1752, he flew his kite just before a thunderstorm to see if the air was charged with electricity. The first hint of the incredible practical applications of electricity did not come until 1831, when Michael Faraday, an Englishman, invented continuous electric current and the essential elements of the electric motor. Others had learned that electricity produces a magnetic field, leading Faraday to discover that a magnetic field could produce electricity. This was the principle of induction: wires wrapped around magnets carried electricity and became the essential element of the dynamo or generator.

Thomas Edison neither discovered electricity nor invented the electric motor, but it is understandable that people think that he did both. His invention of the lightbulb in 1879 was simple enough, but it transformed the world. This device touched people's lives pervasively, seductively, and continuously. But Edison was not only the father of this marvelous invention. Almost at the same time as he invented the electric lightbulb, he invented the institution that would deliver its light to the people—the electric utility.

From the start, the product and its purveyor were so closely identified as to be almost indistinguishable. As the small customer, the city office, and the big factory thirsted for electric power, they became dependent on the electric utility. Because Edison's investors were seeking to profit from his inventions, in the United States more than anywhere else the vital product came from private companies and not from the government. In a characteristically American way, people became dependent on private companies for an essential product. Thus the story of electricity in American life has played out as the story of the power companies and later of the ways in which government has tried to control and guide them.

This story has passed through four phases. The first, from the 1880s to the Great Depression and Franklin D. Roosevelt's New Deal that came as a response to it, was a period when the utilities exercised almost unlimited license and engaged in greedy business practices while spreading the wonders of electricity. In the early days, electric power was used by rapidly growing industry and in urban commerce. The start of the second phase ended many industry abuses and made possible the beginning of electricity's great potential in residential and commercial use. The Roosevelt administration set out to democratize access to electricity by placing government directly in the business. But while Roosevelt's reforms led to a more mature industry providing power to the entire country, they faded in a renewed period of utility dominance. In 1973, the Arab oil embargo awakened the country to its vulnerability in relying on electricity and other energy resources and created the demand that the industry change the way it conducted its business. In this third phase, electricity prices rose high enough to attract the attention of consumers and government. The notion that electric utilities had to be monopolies began to erode. Finally, a little-known milestone was reached in 1992 with the enactment of a single new federal law. The Energy Policy Act, passed in obscurity on the eve of a presidential election, finally ended the long-held belief that the utility business must be conducted by monopolies and mandated the start of competition, the fourth phase in the story of the industry.

Through these phases there were two constants. First, no matter what government might do, the business would be dominated by large, private corporations with enormous power to set the conditions under which they operate. Second, never did consumers, except the largest industrial customers, have any influence over the way the industry developed, over how the power is delivered, or over how much they must pay for it.

Every month in America, a miracle occurs. Tens of millions of people pay their electric bills. In a society in which people increasingly distrust much of what they are told, almost all of them, except industrial customers, pay the bill without knowing the price of the product and usually without even looking at the monthly statement other than to check how much to pay. Electricity customers pay about $24 billion each month. It is an amazing exercise in trust.

Consumers are mistaken, however, if they believe that someone else is looking out for them, that they are getting a good deal, or that there is nothing they can do about it. Their trust is misplaced because, in the vast majority of cases, they are paying too much. They are victims of a system designed to overcharge them—almost since the first customer in New York City paid the first electric bill to Thomas Edison more than 120 years ago.

Each year, American electricity customers in big industry and small homes use more than 3.7 trillion kilowatt-hours of electricity. That is a huge amount and almost unimaginable when one takes into account that the average household uses less than 10,000 kilowatt-hours a year. Americans buy this electricity from utility companies, and they pay an estimated $18 billion a year more than they should.[1] That is equal to the entire annual spending of the state of Colorado.

In a country fearful that terrorists might cut off electric power supplies, most people do not worry about power companies cutting corners and manipulating regulators to improve their profits at the cost of reduced reliability. But electric service is vulnerable because of the failure of the power companies to manage their wires responsibly. When an event like the major blackout of August 2003 occurs, caused by a single utility and spread by the results of poor and selfish management, we hardly need terrorists to reveal just how exposed Americans are.

The electricity Americans get is not as reliable as it should be, and it costs too much.

The reason: American electric companies have always both produced power and exercised power.

1

EDISON'S SECRETARY

A strand of hair—a single strand. On this almost invisible wisp an industry would be founded. Thomas A. Edison, until only a year earlier a relatively unknown inventor toiling in a laboratory in Menlo Park, New Jersey, had discovered that if he could pass electricity over a wire of some sort and do so in the almost complete absence of air, it would glow and give off light. If oxygen were present or if the wire burned too easily, the glow would last for only seconds.

Despite the acclaim that would soon come to him, Edison did not invent this idea. Many others had thought of producing light using electricity. But Edison succeeded in inventing a lightbulb that would last for hours, then days, then months. He did not pursue such knowledge for its own sake. He did it for money. He knew that a durable lightbulb would create an industry from which he and others could draw immense profit.

He was not new as an inventor. First he had invented the stock ticker. Almost by accident and on his first try in 1877, Edison had come up with the first sound recording device, which he dubbed the phonograph. The following year, he set up a company to sell the new apparatus, and he thought he could apply what he had learned from the phonograph to lighting. However much people might like recordings, they needed light. Edison's success with the phonograph and Alexander Graham Bell's telephone patent had awakened the interest of investors looking to profit from new technology. They willingly backed Edison's quest for an electric light. With their money, Edison set out to make a durable incandescent lightbulb and then a no-less-durable electric utility. In the earliest days of the electric industry, Edison, joined by an able assistant who was soon to surpass his master, created a model that would continue even into the twenty-first century.

First, of course, he had to invent the lightbulb. The challenge was to find a wire that would glow and produce light without burning out quickly. He found that a human hair, coated with a variety of substances, yielded positive results, so he kept looking for a wire that would mimic and prolong that experiment. It turned out to be tungsten. He also knew that he needed a vacuum, so he had to come up with a way of evacuating the air from a transparent glass container in which he placed the filament, the word he coined for the wire. Just one year after inventing the phonograph, he was making great progress toward coming up with the right balance of wire, container, and vacuum.

Grosvenor Lowrey, a lawyer friend, took on the task of raising the necessary money to turn the experiment into a commercial product. Lowery went as far as leaking news of Edison's initial successes in order to stimulate market interest, even though they ran the risk that such news might help others beat Edison to the patent. By late 1878, a syndicate had been formed with J. Pierpont Morgan, the leading American banker, as its principal backer. The new company was known as the Edison Electric Light Company, and it would be the ancestor of all of the Edison companies that followed.[2]

Edison's Inventions

The new company needed not only a functioning lightbulb but also everything else necessary to generate electricity and deliver it to people so they could make their new lightbulbs shine. Morgan and his friends expected Edison to invent not only the bulb but all the elements of the system required to create an electric company. Far greater than his inventing the lightbulb was Edison's accomplishment in creating the electric utility.

Before the first utility could begin to operate, Edison had to perfect a generator that would transform the fuel—coal—into electric power. This was the dynamo, a generator that would provide direct current (DC), the same kind of electricity that comes from batteries. The dynamo was the key to the utility. It had to work reliably and be capable of being regulated while in operation. Part of the challenge here was for Edison to find a method for keeping voltage constant. He also had to invent the network of wires called the circuit, along with the fuses and insulation. Just as important was the need to come up with sockets and with switches for turning lights on and off.

If he did all of that, he would have created an electric utility. Or almost. It would only work if the cost of the electricity, including the dynamo, the wires, the bulbs, and the switches, and the profit for Mr. Morgan and his friends added up to less than the cost of lighting with gas. So Edison had to keep the competition in mind from the outset. The phonograph had been much easier, because there had been no real alternative, and he got it right on the first try.

The dynamo was the key to the utility because it would make possible the "central station," a single source of electricity for many customers. Until Edison's invention, all light had been derived from the direct combustion of fuel. Whether the fuel was candles or lantern oil or kerosene or gas, the flame produced light by burning the fuel at the same point. But electricity would be different, because the fuel would burn at a single location—the central station —to create steam to turn a dynamo to create electricity, which would then be carried by wire to the end user. Electricity would separate the customer from the combustion.

By December 1879, Edison could demonstrate that he was going to succeed. He allowed the public to visit his Menlo Park laboratory, now illuminated by electricity. He received the patent in early 1880; the dynamo would take longer. Edison moved to New York City to supervise the construction of the first central station at Pearl Street, the installation of the dynamo, and the laying of wires beneath the city streets.

Less than three years later, on September 4, 1882, the first functioning electric utility was born when the Pearl Street Station in lower Manhattan began selling electricity, carried in underground conduits to fifty-nine customers in neighboring buildings. The price was a then-competitive 24 cents per kilowatt-hour (kWh), an astronomical amount by twenty-first century standards—and even more so when inflation is factored in.

Because of the characteristics of direct current, the utility was limited to serving customers near the central station. At the time, direct current lost voltage, the "power" in electric power, when sent a long distance over wires. Wires conducting the electricity, just like the filaments in lightbulbs, resist this power and grow warm. Power would be converted to heat before reaching the bulb. The limits of direct current's behavior on wires meant that utilities could cover only small areas. As Edison saw the industry, it would consist of many central stations independent from one another and sprinkled across urban areas.

When Edison had ironed out the start-up problems of his New York central station, he began planning for the extension of his utility to other cities. Until the construction of the first central station, Edison had relied entirely on capital from Morgan and his colleagues. The investors, who had poured half a million dollars into the development of the lightbulb and his other electric innovations, had a stranglehold on him. They owned the patents, so he had to pay them for the right to manufacture and sell his own inventions. And they did not like the central station. They wanted to put a generator in each large building that would provide power only to that building. They thought they would get their payoff a lot faster than from the slow development of central stations. They would invest no more. They would go no further than 334 isolated plants, one central station, and one unhappy inventor.

The man who could translate Edison's plan for many central stations to reality now arrived at Edison's office. Samuel Insull was a twenty-one-year-old Englishman recruited to serve as the inventor's secretary. On February 28, 1881, he got off the boat in New York, met Edison, and was hired. By 4:00 AM the following morning, he had been placed in charge of Edison's business assets. Insull had the innate business sense that Edison seemed to lack, and the Wizard of Menlo Park instantly recognized it. This would be one of his most important discoveries. While the inventor would come up with ideas for profitable products, he willingly allowed others to find the money to turn those ideas into reality, though it meant losing control and a large share of the profits. Insull would transform the business from one central electric station serving customers no more than a few city blocks away into a national industry. By the time his career ended, everybody knew what an electric utility was, though many did not like what they saw. Insull created both a successful industry and a national dislike of it.[3]

As Edison began to break with his investors, he sent Insull across the country looking for opportunities for central stations. The young Englishman, who looked barely old enough to be taken seriously, had to struggle with corrupt municipal governments to obtain franchises and often had to outmaneuver local gas companies. He proved adept at the game, which included making required and routine political payoffs. Using his obvious skill in winning these battles, Insull not only obtained many franchises but laid the groundwork for a national industry. Central stations would soon begin operating in more than a score of cities.

Insull's achievements caused the final break with the original investors. At first, Edison's backers wanted isolated plants because of the quick return on their investment. Then, when manufacturing orders for new central stations began to pile up, they wanted to take control of his factories away from Edison. In 1884, after a battle for shareholder support, Edison won, at least for a while.

But the world would not stand still for Edison. Seeking to avoid a labor dispute, he moved his manufacturing operations from New York City to Schenectady and put Insull in charge of the new company, known as Edison General Electric. The plant was enormously successful, and revenues were plowed back into the company to support further expansion. Insull raised funds from a new group of investors, but the company also assumed a huge amount of debt. Morgan was back on the scene, using the burden of debt as a way to force Edison to sell. In 1892, Morgan succeeded, took over the company, and renamed it by simply deleting Edison's name. General Electric (GE), one of America's largest corporations, would prove to be one of its most durable.

Insull Takes Over

Edison the inventor came away from the electric business a wealthy man who went on to add motion pictures to his astounding list of accomplishments. Insull turned down a job offer at GE and set off to create the modern electric industry. His base of operations would be Chicago, where he was hired to head the local central station operation. Until his arrival, the owners of the Edison company there believed that only a relatively few customers would be interested in buying electricity and that the luxury product should be sold at a high price. Insull believed that more money was to be made by selling to many people at lower prices. However, because a central station could serve only a limited number of customers, the fixed costs of the plant—mostly the investment in equipment—were high. As the fixed costs could not be spread over a great many customers, there was no way to bring down the cost of power. At the same time, the price of gaslight was falling. It looked as though the owners were right: the industry should focus on catering to a few large customers.

But Insull was restive; he set out to sell as much electricity as he could at whatever price he could get people to pay. Lacking a good idea of the cost of producing electricity, he was unsure if he was making money but was sure he was capturing customers. He soon came to understand that the heart of a profitable utility was its rates. The cost of the facilities would be spread over the number of units of electricity—the kilowatt-hours—that customers bought. The plant investment was determined by the maximum requirement imposed on the generator by each customer, he thought, though the customer might use that maximum amount during only a few hours of the year.

The manager of the Brighton, England, utility had come up with rates that levied charges based on the maximum amount used by a customer and then cut the rate for all kilowatt-hours after the fixed costs had been recovered. This was the origin of what later came to be known as the two-part rate. The part of the charge that recovered the fixed cost of the plant became the "demand" charge, because it reflected the maximum demand that the customer made on the equipment. The part of the charge that covered the cost of the fuel and any other consumables came to be known as the "energy" charge. The Brighton manager designed an electric meter that would show demand to accompany the meter that showed energy consumption. The demand charge would guarantee that the utility company did not lose money on its capital investment and could also be assured of a profit. The lower energy charge, which included some profit as well, would encourage people to use more electricity. The English utility operator had discovered the notion of "load," the amount of generating capacity required by the customer. His design of rates encouraged people to use more electricity, because once they had covered the demand charge, the cost of each unit of electricity was relatively low. Insull came upon this innovative rate concept when he visited Brighton and was stunned to see the streets strung with blazing lights.

Insull took the Brighton idea and improved it. He did not see "load" alone; he came up with the idea of the "load factor." The more electricity a customer used hour after hour, the lower was not only the cost of the additional kilowatt-hours but also the average cost of each unit consumed. If each customer required that a certain amount of the company's generation be dedicated to meeting his or her maximum requirement, then Insull wanted that customer to operate as close to that peak requirement as much as possible. The percentage of the maximum generating capacity reserved for a customer that was actually used over an extended period—a month or a year—was the customer's load factor. A customer who agreed to use a large part of the facilities required to meet his peak requirement would be entitled to a lower average rate than one with a lower load factor. Insull realized that he could cut deals with individual customers instead of charging all customers the same rate, as had been done in Brighton.

Insull also noticed that two or more customers could share the same equipment if one used its highest share of the generating plant when the other used little, and vice versa. The Chicago Edison company did not need to build enough generation to serve the maximum demand of the sum of the highest requirement of each of its customers; it needed only enough to meet the maximum demand on the system in the heaviest hour. The "load shape" of each customer mattered, and Insull could market effectively and profitably by putting together the highest possible utility company load factor. To accomplish his new rate design and tweak it until it worked to produce the greatest profit, Insull had his staff track and measure customer behavior. Now he knew he was making money. And the rate-making principles that he developed have remained, virtually unchanged, as the basis for today's electric rates.

Insull's objective was to serve as many customers as possible, but direct current, which could not travel more than a mile from the central station, created problems. Insull's first solution was to build many central stations and purchase other stations from companies serving areas adjacent to his own. But in 1886 a legendary inventor almost in a class with Edison, George Westinghouse, came up with the transformer, a piece of equipment that led to alternating current (AC), which could be transmitted over long distances, even hundreds of miles. Using the ideas of inventor Nikola Tesla, a Croatian immigrant, Westinghouse realized that the higher the voltage of power, the further it could travel. By using the transformer he could increase the voltage, transmit the power, and then use another transformer to lower the voltage again for service to the end user. At the time, DC could not be stepped up to the higher voltage needed for long-distance transmission. Edison himself was furious with Westinghouse, going so far as to denigrate AC by suggesting that the New York State electric chair should be powered by AC and renamed the "Westinghouse Chair."[4]

But Insull would be the best customer for AC, and in adopting it, he departed with no apparent reluctance from Edison's position. For Insull, a single central station could now serve many more customers based on the same investment. He also realized that AC allowed him to reach beyond the densely packed urban market.

The combination of his rate design and the use of AC meant that Insull was now ready to move beyond serving big-city offices and apartments to the much larger loads of industrial customers and areas outside urban centers. His first targets were the traction companies, the operators of urban trolley cars. Because he could combine their demand with the loads of other customers and provide them electricity more economically than they could by operating alone, they signed on with Commonwealth Electric Company, as Insull's Chicago company was now called. These developments called for a greater ability to generate power than was possible with the steam engines the utility was using.

When Edison General Electric had been taken over, Insull vowed to get even. He decided that what he needed now was an enormous steam turbine AC generator and that GE would be the company to build it. Overcoming GE's reluctance by threatening to go to England to have such a generator built, Insull proposed to build the new turbine as a joint development project between GE and his own company. Insull now called the tune, and the president of GE danced to it.

With the AC generator Insull could not be stopped. While he did not always succeed in penetrating rural areas, he bought companies that extended his domain from Missouri to Maine and soon had operating companies in thirteen states. Not only did Insull become the dominant baron of the electric business, but his model was followed by others across the country, including the other Edison companies.

While building his empire, Insull drew on his experience in convincing local governments to allow him to place central stations in their communities. He recognized that he needed political support for his plans and so he devoted much of his efforts to cultivating politicians. Often he succeeded, but when he failed, he reacted intemperately. His occasional fury with some politicians, never forgotten by those he opposed, would prove to have a significant effect on the development of the electric industry.

His signal success with politicians was in perpetrating the great myth underlying the electric business in the twentieth century. He convinced state legislatures and city councils that electric service ought to be a monopoly. When he went into an area to site a central station, he sought and frequently obtained an exclusive franchise. He would usually not agree to do business without one. In theory, an area without electric service could be opened to competition to see who would be the prevailing supplier or to allow several companies each to serve part of the territory. In reality, politicians were willing to give the great Edison's designated representative the monopoly he demanded in return for favors or simply because they could be convinced to trust the Edison name over all others.

Electric service came to be known as a "natural" monopoly because it was unacceptable to have two sets of power lines along the sides of the street. The basis for this belief was the unquestioning acceptance of the notion that an electric utility should both generate the power and deliver it to the customer—Thomas Edison's model. Although manufacturing was coming to be separated from distribution—Sears, Roebuck and Co. had never made every product it sold from its catalog and delivered to its customers —Edison had started a "vertically integrated" utility, in which a single company produced, sold, and delivered the product. Insull sold the need for the Edison central station along with the rest of the utility as if it were the most natural thing in the world, and everybody agreed. Strictly for business reasons, Insull demanded treatment as a monopoly and then turned the idea into the widely held belief that electric utilities were "natural monopolies," an article of faith that lasted in the United States until 1978.

As Insull's empire spread, he was wise enough to understand that the idea of a natural monopoly was fragile and could begin to cause a political backlash in state legislatures if it went completely unchecked. The Sherman Act, designed to tame the monopolies, had been passed late in the nineteenth century and it, too, could cause trouble. What Insull needed was political insulation from efforts to withdraw his monopoly rights. The solution was regulation.

The federal government's Interstate Commerce Commission, created in 1887 to regulate railroads, was the first American regulatory body. But Insull preferred to promote the idea of state regulation, a reasonable idea in the early twentieth century because utility companies were small and did not often have customers in more than one state. Besides, it would be easier to influence the new state bodies as they appeared on the scene than it would be to influence a federal regulator. Insull's support of state regulation fitted well with his demands for a monopoly within a state's boundaries.

Out of the combination of the growth of the electric monopoly and the appearance of state regulators came the "regulatory bargain." It was seductively simple: the state would give the utility the exclusive right to operate in a specific area, and in return, the utility as a monopoly would agree to have its rates set by the regulator. Although Edison had started out to compete with gaslight companies, the success of his invention had virtually eliminated competition, so a substitute was needed. The state utility regulator would become the "surrogate of competition." Substituting the regulator's judgment for the interplay of forces in the marketplace would assure customers that they were getting the benefits of the kind of pricing they would have experienced in a competitive market.

But as state regulation started, legislatures were easily persuaded by Insull and his allies that the rules of the competitive game required that the regulator not represent the customers' interest but rather the "public interest." This concept meant that at the same time as it kept rates as low as possible for the customers, the regulator had to insure a fair return on investment to the utility shareholders to induce further investment in the expansion of electric service.

Regulation began to appear in the first quarter of the twentieth century, long after Insull had already developed and promoted the operating principles of both electric utilities and electric rates. The small state regulatory bodies began their lives at a significant disadvantage compared with the utility lawyers who came before them seeking franchises and rate approvals. The regulatory "bargain" was a good deal for the utilities. For one thing, they wanted to keep rates down to attract new customers, the key to bringing in new investment. For another, they did not really have to slash rates, because alternatives to the electric light were increasingly unacceptable to customers. Finally, their smooth and skilled lawyers had the field almost entirely to themselves in arguing for substantial profit margins, because almost no representatives of consumer interests took part in the regulatory proceedings.

Across the heavily populated East and Midwest, small utilities continued to take root. The high-voltage transmission line was still well off in the future, so utilities needed only to focus on generators and distribution wires to bring the power to nearby customers. Some utilities grew up near rivers, which could be dammed and the force of falling water harnessed to turn a turbine. Wall Street investors started to make attractive offers to the local businessmen who had launched these small companies. Gradually, the small utilities began to consolidate, a process that would go on for more than fifty years. Because of his superior knowledge of the electric business, Insull could strike deals with the new owners, who had underestimated the complexity of owning and managing the properties they had acquired. Insull's empire expanded as far west as Oklahoma. He managed to accomplish what nobody else had: becoming the nationally dominant owner of facilities in a specific sector and operating them as a monopoly. The railroads, the oil companies, and manufacturers had all failed to obtain such a grip on the economy or were under constant threat of the application of the Sherman Act. But not Insull.

The American electric industry now took shape. While some communities had started their utilities as public undertakings, most utilities had been private companies, and many became part of larger entities. Though they might be owned by a company in another state, they were subject only to state regulation. In short, the electric industry was becoming a major force in the United States—free to do as it wished and much of it under the control of a shrewd Englishman, Samuel Insull.

The Origins of Reform

The 1920s saw the beginnings of a reform movement brought on by popular concern over the excesses of the corporate giants that were gaining dominance over the American economy, enriching their owners at the expense of essentially unprotected customers. In

1924, the reformist former governor of Wisconsin, Robert M. LaFollette, ran for president on the Progressive Party ticket. He was rebelling against what he considered the domination of the economy by less than a hundred "industrialists," including Insull. He argued that they not only controlled the economy but stood to control the government as well. Although he won only about a sixth of the popular vote, LaFollette had much of the effect he desired. If the progressive movement were not to gain strength, a government dominated by the Republican Party, against which "Fighting Bob" LaFollette had revolted, would have to yield to some of the progressives' demands.

Regulation had been merely symbolic when Insull first supported it, but the reform movement reflected growing consumer dissatisfaction with the way the investor-owned utilities were treating them. Without fully understanding the utility business and how rates worked, some customers resented the ability of the power companies to reap big profits at customer expense and apparently with little control being exercised over them. Insull, the dominant leader of utilities across the country, came to represent what people most worried about.

The first step by government to impose more regulation was the creation of the Federal Power Commission (FPC) in 1920. Early in the twentieth century, long-distance transmission had become practicable, making it possible to carry power generated at dams on remote waterways to urban areas. Damming rivers to generate electricity affected the broad public interest, and Congress decided the federal government should control such dams. Though the new agency had little enforcement authority, Congress asserted for the first time a federal regulatory interest in the electric business by basing the FPC's role on the national government's authority over navigable waterways. The FPC would issue licenses for the dams but it would not control the rates charged for the power generated at the sites of the dams. Although for many years the commission would be seen as a friend of the utilities, its creation was the foundation of an ever increasing federal regulatory role.

LaFollette was not alone. Other reformers began attacking the utilities. Nebraska senator George Norris, a progressive Republican like LaFollette, claimed in 1929 that utilities were overcharging their customers $750 million a year ($8.285 billion in 2004 dollars). Insull derided Norris's estimate, claiming that somewhat dubious Federal Trade Commission (FTC) figures showed that total electricity sales were less than the amount of the alleged overcharge. But the press picked up on these charges, and during 1929 and 1930, Insull found himself under enormous public pressure to account for the wealth he had amassed from the utility business. Edison, having achieved virtual sainthood and having been long removed from utility operations, was unscathed by the growing attacks on the industry.

Despite his ability to deal with politicians through a combination of flattery and financial muscle, Insull's political relationships began to unravel. The first mistake he made was minor but drew unfavorable attention. On the advice of W. S. Wyman, the man in charge of his Central Maine Power Company, Insull took on the state's Fernald Law, which prohibited the export to other states of power from Maine's hydroelectric resources. The law was almost certainly unconstitutional, but it was popular, and Insull was roundly attacked in the press for trying to change it.

His next error was in 1930, at the World Power Conference in Berlin, where the American ambassador was scheduled to deliver a speech asserting that U.S. utility companies were charging fifteen times the true cost of generating power. Insull was in Germany and succeeded in bullying the ambassador into withdrawing the speech.

When the story broke, Insull was made to look as though he was attempting to control a U.S. official. His allies rallied to his defense with the weak argument that the real value of electricity was in its transmission and distribution. They were unpersuasive, because such costs are only a small fraction of the cost of generation.

Insull's biggest mistake was an attack by his brother Martin against then–New York governor Franklin D. Roosevelt. Like Norris, Roosevelt had charged that the profits of the utility companies were unjustified. Even more ominously for Insull, Roosevelt made it clear that he did not like holding companies, the very structure that Insull had used to build his national empire. A holding company owns and controls other companies. Through Insull's ownership of such holding companies as Middle West and Insull Utility Investments (IUI), which in turn owned utility companies in many states, Insull could dominate the electric industry. Counterattacking, Martin Insull claimed that Roosevelt was motivated not merely by political grandstanding but by his bitterness at have been turned down for a job with a New York utility. This intemperate blast was sure to rankle with the proud man at whom it was aimed. Insull would sorely regret having created an enemy in Roosevelt.

Insull's Fall

Meanwhile, Insull did not suspect that forces beyond his control would bring about a major change in the structure of the industry he had built. His success had happened so swiftly and so massively that he had come to believe that he was invulnerable and that attacks from "misguided" reformers like LaFollette, Norris, and Roosevelt could be safely ignored. He was soon to be proven wrong.

The Great Depression, which began in October 1929, showed that a meteoric rise in business could be followed by a similarly dramatic collapse. The Insull empire, it turned out, was a house of cards, and the Depression provided the push that toppled it. The number of investor-owned electric companies had reached 6,500 by the beginning of the 1920s. But then the number began to decline as utilities merged. Even more important was the growth of holding companies. Operating companies came under the control of holding companies that were themselves under the control of even more holding companies. Sometimes there were ten layers between the actual owners and the operating utilities. At the top were only a few companies, with three of them responsible for 45 percent of the power generation in the United States. Insull's was the biggest.

To complicate further the corporate enterprises that Insull and others controlled, their holding companies became involved in a variety of businesses, many of which had nothing to do with electric utilities. Revenues derived from customers at regulated rates—which supposedly limited the profits of the operating companies but which actually allowed excess profits to be kept hidden—could be diverted into these other, unregulated businesses. In theory, if a utility made more money than the regulators had allowed, the utility's rates should be cut. In practice, the excess revenues were hidden from regulators and available to invest in businesses producing no savings to the customers whose money was used.

The confusing array of holding companies helped Insull and his colleagues avoid serious regulatory scrutiny. While most states had created utilities commissions by the 1920s, they could not keep up with the holding companies, much less effectively regulate them. Customers were given the false impression that utilities were being regulated, when in reality regulators were befuddled and outgunned by the power companies. The state commissions' staffs lacked the expertise to understand the intricate financial structures built by the utilities. The utility holding companies engaged in massive self-dealing, with the regulated operating companies being charged high prices for supplies from other entities under the same ownership. The affiliated suppliers, not the regulated utilities, performed most of the utility services, which might include fuel supply, customer billing, engineering, and construction. Regulators failed to understand the underlying business relationships and lacked sufficient staff and skill to probe whether utilities' costs were out of line. As a result, regulators failed in their essential role: protecting customers from excessively high rates. Rates had declined over the years as the power companies took on more customers, and these decreases masked the overcharges.

State regulators also overlooked a fundamental change that was taking place in the economic structure of the business. Insull had led everybody to focus on the economies that could be realized by adept use of the load factor. But their attention had been drawn away from the Brighton discovery that after the fixed costs of facilities had been paid, the cost of additional kilowatt-hours would be less. As utilities had grown under the tutelage of holding companies, economies of scale that would have been unimaginable a decade or two earlier began to be achieved, so that the cost of generating the last kilowatt-hour was markedly less than the cost of generating the first one. Regulators overlooked these savings and allowed the utilities to overcollect from their customers. The illusion of regulation was particularly harmful because electric companies were now full-fledged and powerful monopolies. In 1928, the Federal Trade Commission reported on the nefarious practices of electric holding companies. This report was a more likely source for Roosevelt's attacks in New York than was his past personal employment situation, but it led to no immediate action.

The big utilities' scheme to overcharge customers might have continued for decades longer, were it not for the Great Depression. With businesses failing and personal incomes falling, customers cut back their use of costly electricity. As customers' revenues declined, so did those of the electric companies. Even more seriously, the holding companies received too little income to meet their debt obligations.

Insull had always used loans, even from the New York bankers he detested, to fund his companies' growth and to insure that he could maintain control through his ownership of much of the stock. He sought to avoid Edison's errors but nevertheless placed himself in the path of the same kind of corporate misfortune that had wrested Edison General Electric from its founder. Insull thought the lenders would not desert him this time. But the cosmic chaos of the Depression was accompanied by the collapse of the banking system. Even as the situation grew worse, Insull expected that he could keep his creditors at bay simply because they would prefer to bet on his recovery rather than forcing him out of business with their calls for repayment of his loans. But the banks could not wait out hard times because they themselves were going under.

Underestimating the depth of the crisis, he struggled, almost in panic, to come up with the money to pay off the loans. The stock in his companies plunged in free fall. The collapse was characteristic of what was happening to holding companies, many of which were deeply in debt. Not only were lenders unable to collect on loans and forced out of business, but shareholders, believing, like Insull, that the bubble would never burst, were wiped out. The fall of the Insull empire took many people down with it.

Insull's downfall resulted from greed. He had understood early in the development of the industry that by lowering prices he could make electric lighting accessible to all people and not merely a luxury for the rich. He had recognized that by selling vast amounts of power with a low profit margin and by taking advantage of the inherent economic advantages of the power business, he could reward investors handsomely. But once people had become dependent on electric lighting, he increased his profits, and they had nowhere else to turn. And he could cement his position by expanding rapidly and gaining even greater control if he resorted to debt financing. Regulators would simply be the window dressing he needed to make it all look as though it worked in the customer's interest. A little creative accounting under the supervision of the man Edison had quickly understood had a knack for numbers was all that was needed to do the job. But when the market collapsed, so did the scheme. If there had been no dose of economic reality imposed by the Depression, Insull might have been able to keep up his march toward complete dominance of the industry.

Looking back more than seventy years later, Arthur Levitt, a former chairman of the Securities and Exchange Commission, compared a modern financial disaster to Insull's meltdown:

> Enron's fall brings to mind another massive bankruptcy. The company I refer to was one of the largest enterprises in the nation, and it collapsed under the weight of its multilayered, interconnected corporate structure—a structure supported, of course, by very creative accounting. This company's fall touched hundreds of thousands of investors. Newspapers called it the biggest business failure in the history of the world, and this historic moment happened in 1931. The company was Insull Utility Investments (IUI), founded by Samuel Insull, a onetime private secretary to Thomas Edison.[5]

Arrogance and manipulation had finally brought down Sam Insull, the man who had taken Edison's inspiration and turned it into an industry. After the worst had happened, as often is the case, the government would move to adopt rules to prevent the same kind of abuses from happening again. As for Insull, his financial failure and the bankruptcy of his companies were followed by charges of fraud and embezzlement. At first, he fled the country to seek refuge in Europe, but he eventually returned to face trial in Chicago. He claimed that he had done—better than most, to be sure—only what was legal and common practice. Though he was acquitted, he never recovered his reputation. The *Chicago Times* reflected the general opinion: "Insull and his fellow defendants— not guilty; the old order—guilty. That was the Insull defense, and the jury agreed with it."[6] A harsher verdict, but probably no less accurate, was pronounced by *The Nation* magazine, which found that the outcome "illustrates once more the difficulty of sending a rich man to jail, no matter how flagrant his crime."[7]

Power: From Source to Customer

Most electricity is produced by generators, devices that put electrons into motion by the rotation of one magnet past another. Electrons carry an electrical charge. Their flow over wires is called electric current. Current can be either direct or alternating. Direct current is a continuous and steady flow of electrons in the same direction. Alternating current is a flow of electrons that rapidly switches direction. In the United States, almost all power is delivered by an alternating current that changes direction 60 times a second.

The maximum output of any generator is its capacity. Because electricity customers may require the use of the capacity or a lesser amount of the total generating capability of the generator, their call on the generator's capacity is called demand. Directly or indirectly, they pay for the capacity they need to have reserved for their use by means of a demand charge. Capacity is measured in units called watts, named after the British inventor James Watt, and most customer demand is calculated in kilowatts or 1,000 watts. Customers must also pay for the electrons they use, called energy. Their consumption of energy is calculated as the amount of their demand over the course of an hour and is measured in kilowatt-hours. Large amounts of power are measured as megawatts (1,000 kilowatts).

A useful analogy is water. It can be stored in a water tower, whose size must be at least as great as the maximum demand for water at any moment. Customers must pay for the water tower, and this payment constitutes their demand charge. They must also pay for the quantity of water they consume, and that is equivalent to the energy charge.

Large amounts of power for use by many customers travel over heavy-duty wires from the generator. Voltage is the strength of the electrical source and can be understood as the force in electricity that makes it move across wires. It was named after the Italian inventor Alessandro Volta. These large lines are high-voltage and constitute transmission. A network of transmission lines is called the grid. Voltage may be increased or reduced by the use of transformers.

Power may pass over transmission lines owned by several companies. If the customer's bill reflects the costs of paying each company separately, the process is called pancaking, as the transmission rates are stacked on top of one another. The creation of larger market areas can reduce or eliminate pancaking.

Power passes from the transmission system onto lower-voltage wires that carry it to customers' sites. The lower-voltage system is called distribution. Through the use of transformers, power is reduced in voltage from hundreds of thousands of volts (1,000 volts = 1 kilovolt) at the generator to 110 volts at the home.

Electric utilities have traditionally included generation, transmission, and distribution functions. They also include metering, billing, and other customer services. Restructuring is meant to allow some of these functions to be performed by nonutilities.

2

POWER POPULISM

On October 21, 1931, electric lights all across the United States dimmed for one minute—not as the result of the Depression or bankruptcies in the industry but to mark the passing of Thomas A. Edison, the man who had started it all, dead at eighty-four. Although he had profited from Insull's industry, his reputation as the preeminent American scientist and inventor was untarnished. Utility companies across the country would continue to bear his name as a badge of honor. When Insull died seven years later, he remained, though credited for his business innovations and despite the efforts of his supporters, in disgrace because of the harm he had done to customers, investors, and public confidence.

Insull had lived to see the revenge of two of the people he had scorned—Senator George W. Norris, the Nebraska Republican, and President Franklin D. Roosevelt, the New York Democrat. State regulators had proven inadequate to the task of dealing with giant and multilayered utility companies, so federal action was necessary to bring the utilities under control. Roosevelt's New Deal, a political movement with which many GOP progressives, including Norris, felt comfortable, responded to public clamor for action against large corporations. A majority existed in Congress to resist the national utilities. Washington was at last ready to act and to make the regulatory bargain less one-sided and more fair to customers.

PUHCA Breaks the Holding Companies

In 1935, Congress passed the Public Utility Holding Company Act (PUHCA).[8] Under PUHCA, holding companies were banned from being more than twice removed from the operating companies, meaning that a holding company could still own a holding company that in turn owned a utility company. Ownership was defined as at least a 10 percent interest. No companies were grandfathered against these requirements, so the provision was known as the "Death Sentence Clause" for many electric companies. All electric and gas utility holding companies were required to register with the newly created Securities and Exchange Commission (the SEC). This New Deal agency was given broad powers over the creation of holding companies and over their activities. It would regulate mergers, acquisitions, and the issuance of securities, and would review books and records kept according to the agency's dictates. Operating companies were forbidden to make loans to their parent companies, and all holding company financing was to be subject to SEC approval. Utility holding companies were limited to a single integrated and regulated business, although they were permitted to operate; across state or international borders. They could not freely enter other businesses and had to keep utility customer finances segregated from other holding company investments.

While such changes might seem unexceptional from the vantage point of the twenty-first century, they caused a revolutionary change in the industry. For the first time, strict and better-informed regulation of the electric industry could take place. Because of the scrutiny of utility holding companies and the SEC's complex requirements applied at the federal level, PUHCA would drive regulation back to the states, this time allowing them to deal with the more manageable-sized entities that were not controlled by interstate holding companies and, Washington hoped, to respond to public concerns and not merely to sugarcoat industry practices. In effect, PUHCA was a form of trust-busting because it marked the apparent end of the interstate electric utility. Franklin D. Roosevelt, maligned by the Insull brothers while he was New York governor, had his revenge, though probably only his harshest critics assumed that PUHCA was an act of retaliation.

In the wake of PUHCA, most holding companies survived at the state level and avoided doing business across state borders. But the law required that the states regulate them, making inevitable the extension of utility regulation to all states. Many utilities, among them some of the largest in the country, chose to keep a simple corporate structure and avoid holding companies altogether. By the 1990s, in a mature industry, there were only twelve electric holding companies engaged in interstate operations under SEC control, controlling 18 percent of all electric utility assets. The remainder, whether or not holding companies, did not involve ownership across state borders. In an industry that had been on its way to domination by three holding companies, more than two hundred investor-owned electric companies now controlled about 88 percent of utility assets.

Government Gets into the Game

If the passage of PUHCA marked the turning point in the evolution of the electric industry from its purely entrepreneurial origins to a more regulated existence, the new law was only one of a series of changes meant to reshape the industry. The initial step under the New Deal had been the creation in 1933 of the Tennessee Valley Authority (TVA).[9] This entirely new entity put the federal government itself into the power business and was characteristic of the broad sweep of innovation that Roosevelt brought to Washington to cope with the crisis brought on by the Depression. The TVA combined many elements of New Deal policies: direct government intervention in the economy, government action to compensate for private-sector deficiencies, aid for disadvantaged people, and massive outpourings of funds for capital equipment to stimulate the economy.

Despite Insull's claims that he would bring electricity to rural areas through his vast utilities, he and other barons of the industry had cherry-picked their service territories and ignored less densely settled areas where there were fewer customers for each mile of line. The core of the Deep South was dotted with small towns deep in poverty. They had almost no access to electricity. The TVA would do more than bring electric light; it would transform a society.

The TVA set the pattern for change. As a federal power administration, it would use funds from the entire country to subsidize service for disadvantaged areas. It would bring power to rural areas. It would be a utility, generating, transmitting, and delivering electricity to customers. It would not be subject to regulation but would set its own rules. And, like the holding companies, it would acquire existing utilities. All of these measures would bring enormous benefit to the rural South. But this pattern would also be the basis for setting region against region and plunging the federal government, immune from bankruptcy, into the depths of debt on a scale that Insull had known. The pattern was simply for government to do what the holding companies had done—this time for the benefit of the public.

The TVA's principal sponsor was Senator George Norris. He had come to believe that investor-owned utilities could never operate in the customer's interest and that utilities owned by the people or their government were the only solution. Norris simply removed the profit motive from the utility business. This was a kind of retaliation against the coldhearted power barons. Norris went as far as to bring about in Nebraska, the state he represented, a change unlike any other in the United States. From his day onward, there have been no investor-owned electric utilities in Nebraska.

The TVA was unique in its scope of activities, but it led to the creation in 1935 of the Bonneville Power Administration (BPA)[10] in the Pacific Northwest. The BPA was followed by a string of federal power administrations heavily concentrated in the West and Alaska. Each would transmit and market power generated at federal dams. Each would become the dominant force in its local power market and would set the market price. Each would depend heavily on federal financing.

Norris was also the sponsor of the legislation creating the Rural Electrification Administration (REA). Its goal was similar to the TVA's. It would provide low-cost loans to cooperatives formed to provide electric service in the most sparsely populated areas of the country. Investor-owned utilities simply would not serve such remote locations, but these areas were too scattered to merit federal power administrations. The REA would eventually serve cooperatives in forty-seven states.

The crowning blow to the old ways of business came with the passage of the Federal Power Act[11] in 1935. As early as 1920, the FPC, composed of heads of several government departments, had been created to regulate the construction of electricity-generating dams on the navigable waterways of the United States. By 1930, the agency's staff members, who had been loaned to it by other government departments, were assigned directly as the staff of the fledgling agency. But it would not be until 1935, with the passage of the Federal Power Act, that the federal government began to regulate the electric business.

The New Deal involved the federal government in the industry in three complementary ways: PUHCA stopped the abuses of the past; the TVA, the REA, and the other federal power-marketing agencies made the government itself a player in the market; and the Federal Power Act gave government the beginnings of regulatory power over the investor-owned utilities.

In the reform era, the FPC became an independent regulatory body with a bipartisan five-member board named by the president specifically for the purpose of regulation. The members no longer represented government departments. Based on the authority of the Commerce Clause of the Constitution, over time the FPC gained the responsibility of dealing with transmission—because electrons flowed across state lines—and wholesale transactions among investor-owned utilities. Companies were operating across state lines, but the Supreme Court had ruled in the *Attleboro* case that one state could not examine a utility's assets in another state.[12] By giving the FPC jurisdiction over multistate transactions, Congress closed the "Attleboro gap." The FPC assumed the responsibility for setting transmission rates. The remainder of the regulatory responsibility was left to the states, whose most important task was to set the rates customers were charged. The passage of the Federal Power Act not only served to begin federal regulation of electric utilities but it also stimulated states, some of which had barely launched a system to control their utilities, to expand and improve their own regulation.

Like the other pieces of reform legislation, the Federal Power Act was meant to fix a past mistake—in this case, making sure that there would never be another Sam Insull. No matter that his empire had crumbled of its own weight; he had been responsible for excessive rates for customers and huge losses for hapless investors. The idea that electricity needed a federal regulator that could reach across state lines was caused more by Insull than by any other single person. He had recognized that purely symbolic and often easily influenced regulation limited to the state level left him the opportunity to create national utilities. The Roosevelt Brain Trust, the president's brilliant circle of advisors, concluded that only the federal government could combat such a scheme.

Despite the marked improvement embodied in the Federal Power Act, it was far from a panacea. The states were reluctant to cede any regulatory authority, which they had always considered their exclusive domain, to the FPC. For example, for many years they claimed that, because they had the right to set utility rates, they could refuse to allow FPC-approved costs to flow through to customers. In this, as in several other important aspects of its authority, the FPC had to turn to the U.S. Supreme Court for decisions confirming that because federal law prevails over state law whenever there is a conflict, the Federal Power Act trumped state authority.

Nor would the utilities, even in their reduced scope of action, concede that the FPC could limit what they could do. Here, knowledge was power, and so was political clout. The utilities knew the electric business, but the federal bureaucrats still had much to learn. The regulatory process depended heavily on information that could come only from the power companies. As for the five commissioners, they came to their jobs through the political process and were often more adept at making the right patronage connections than in understanding the right electrical interconnections.

The utilities could still be helpful to candidates, so the companies could indirectly exert influence in the selection of the new federal regulators.

Other factors muted the effect of the new federal regulation. The Depression was weighing down the economy, and no federal agency could afford to be overly tough on companies functioning all across the country that provided good jobs even at times of high unemployment. Because they were essential, utilities were a sound investment. Although the collapse of the Insull empire had destroyed many investors, electric utilities became the investment of choice for the proverbial widows and orphans. When Roosevelt's "Dr. New Deal" gave way to "Dr. Win-the-War," as he called the drive to win World War II, there was added reason to help companies whose operations were vital to the war effort. The new laws had done the job of taming the multistate electric utility, but there was no need to throttle it to the point that economic recovery, a stable return for people on fixed incomes, and mobilization for war would suffer. The FPC represented a new phase in the evolution of the electric industry, but it was more promise than progress.

The direct action of the federal government itself did more to bring down electric rates than did the Federal Power Act. The TVA, the BPA, and the Rural Electrification Act[13] were all steps toward publicly provided power, where there would be no investor and the taxpayer would be either the lender or the guarantor of the loans of others. The bypassing of investors brought power to previously unserved areas on a not-for-profit basis and acted as a yardstick against which neighboring investor-owned utilities might be measured. As a result, rates generally went down in these areas. New Deal regulation might be frustrated by an array of opposing forces, but massive New Deal direct spending on electric facilities could not fail to produce results.

There was also a massive loophole. The Northeast, which would continue to have the highest rates in the country, contributed to the subsidies that made power administrations possible but received none of the federal largesse. The northeastern states had to satisfy themselves with repeated promises that federal power would be priced based on its true cost, promises that seldom turned into reality. Over time, the disparity in electricity costs would take its toll; the migration of the textile industry from New England to the South was one result. In the areas that were the main targets of the federal power administrations, many of which were also the hotbeds of the reform effort, rates declined, and the need for the FPC to take on the utilities was reduced.

The FPC had been given jurisdiction over wholesale electric transactions, those between one utility and a second utility, which served the end-use customers through retail sales. Many wholesale customers were either municipal electrics or rural cooperatives. Some of them came to believe that the FPC was hostile to their interests and likely to favor the investor-owned utilities that it regulated. This grievance would persist for decades. This presumed bias was taken as yet another piece of evidence that the FPC was disappointing the reformist expectations that had led to its creation. Only with President Kennedy's FPC appointments in 1961 would the commission begin to shed its image as a friend of the utilities it regulated.

Strengthened by their role in the war effort, the utilities returned to a position of considerable power in the states in the postwar period. Perhaps they could no longer aspire to national status, but they could exploit their local bases. State regulators remained poorly equipped to deal with many complex utility issues and were frequently complacent if not compliant. Roosevelt's New Deal and Harry Truman's Fair Deal gave way to Dwight D, Eisenhower's probusiness administration; utilities again had a friend in the White House. No complaints came from consumers, because rates seemed reasonable and, with successive recessions, increased little from year to year. While the changes that Roosevelt had brought about were not undone, they were frozen in time.

Despite the New Deal reforms and initiatives, it would not be federal government action nor even improved regulation that would cause the greatest changes in the electric industry as it had been created and developed by Edison and Insull. These changes started with the oil embargo of 1973 to 1974 imposed by the Organization of Petroleum Exporting Countries (OPEC), then mainly an Arab producers' organization.

Acts and Agencies

The history of the electric industry has been marked by several landmark laws and the creation of national and international agencies.

BPA: Bonneville Power Administration, a federal agency generating and marketing power in the Pacific Northwest.

DOE: Department of Energy, a federal agency created in 1978 as part of the National Energy Policy to consolidate U.S. government activities in the energy sector.

EPAct: Energy Policy Act of 1992, which provided for industry restructuring. The same name was used for the energy law passed in 2005, a part of which is the Electricity Modernization Act, designed to improve regulation of transmission reliability. The 2005 law repealed **PUHCA** and weakened **PURPA**.

ERO: See **NERC**.

FERC: Federal Energy Regulatory Commission, a federal agency created in 1978 as part of the National Energy Policy as an independent energy regulator within **DOE** to replace the Federal Power Commission

FPA: Federal Power Act, adopted in 1935 to establish the regulatory authority of the Federal Power Commission (FPC) over portions of the electric industry.

FPC: Federal Power Commission, a federal agency, originally an interagency body with authority over water power, which in 1935 became the federal energy regulatory body.

Fuel Use Act: Federal law, adopted in 1978 to prevent the use of natural gas to generate electricity in new generators. Later repealed.

NERC: North American Electric Reliability Council, created by the industry after the 1965 blackout to provide for voluntary self-regulation to improve reliability; later slated to become the Electricity Reliability Organization, an independent body under **FERC** supervision to administer mandatory transmission reliability standards.

NGA: Natural Gas Act, adopted in 1935, giving the FPC broad powers over the natural gas industry.

NECPA: National Energy Conservation Policy Act, passed in 1978, requiring electric utilities to undertake energy conservation measures.

OPEC: Organization of Petroleum Exporting Countries, grouping Arab, African, and Latin-American oil exporters, initially dominated by the Arab members.

PUHCA: Public Utility Holding Company Act, adopted in 1935 to break up the large holding companies dominating the electric industry and to prevent their recurrence.

PURPA: Public Utility Regulatory Policies Act, adopted in 1978 as part of the National Energy Policy to require utilities to purchase power from nonutility sources using renewable and other resources to reduce reliance on imported oil.

REA: Rural Electrification Administration, created in 1935 to provide low-cost loans to cooperatives established to serve sparsely settled areas avoided by investor-owned utilities. Later renamed Rural Utility Services.

SEC: Securities and Exchange Commission, created in 1933 to regulate the securities industry and administer **PUHCA**.

TVA: Tennessee Valley Authority, created in 1933 as the first federal agency to produce, transmit, and sell electric power. It had a major economic impact in the South.

3

THE EXILE OF REDDY KILOWATT

O n October 6, 1973, Egyptian and Syrian forces launched a surprise attack on Israel on the Jewish holy day of Yom Kippur. After suffering initial losses, the Israeli armed forces counterattacked. The Soviet Union intervened to assist the Arab states, and on October 12 and 13, the United States sent massive airlifts of military equipment to the Israelis. The Israeli forces advanced across the Sinai toward the Suez Canal and crossed it. The Arab attack collapsed, leaving the attackers even weaker than before.

Military force against Israel having failed, the final counterattack was launched against the United States, Israel's strongest supporter, and its backers in Europe. It came not from Egypt or Syria but from the Arab OPEC members. On October 17, oil exports from Arab states to the United States were halted, and the prices charged Europeans were increased.

At the time, much electricity was generated using oil, especially in the densely populated eastern United States. Until 1950, the United States, itself a major oil producer, had been self-sufficient in energy resources. By 1973, however, it relied on oil imports for 35 percent of its needs. A parallel and worrisome development on the supply side was that Arab states, whose oil production and distribution had long been under the management of American and British companies, were taking increasing control over their own resources. OPEC was created in 1960 but had been largely ignored by the United States and Europe. From 1973, OPEC could no longer be ignored.

The American government ordered emergency measures to reduce energy consumption, but conservation was something new for consumers. Long lines waited at gas stations, though gasoline had quadrupled in price. The economy could not adjust quickly enough, and the United States and Europe paid the price for their support of Israel by suffering through a severe recession. But OPEC could not maintain the embargo indefinitely; its members depended on revenues from the American market. In March 1974, the embargo was ended.

Electricity customers began to feel the effect of the embargo soon after it started. Utility rates had been set in regulatory proceedings based upon an analysis of the costs of producing and delivering the power. But they could not accommodate the sudden increase in the cost of one of the principal fuels used to generate electricity. Oil often served as the benchmark for other fuels, whose prices also rose. State regulators began to apply "fuel adjustment clauses" or similar mechanisms that would allow the utilities to pass along to their customers virtually automatically any increase in their fuel costs. These regulatory devices were added to the usual rates, so customers saw a sharp increase in their bills, although many state regulators created a lag in cost recovery by ordering utilities to borrow a part of the funds needed to pay fuel bills. The price run-up and unprecedented messages from the utilities and government calling for conservation brought to an end the electricity binge that started in the days of Insull.

Following the embargo, the federal government began to adopt new policies to protect energy users, including utility customers, from the vulnerability they had suddenly experienced in 1973. The following year, Congress voted to authorize a prohibition on the use of natural gas or oil to generate power, at least at new plants. Without the use of these fossil fuels, new power sources were expected to be powered by renewable resources. Though oil was never banned, this piece of legislation, reflecting the embargo panic, was the first major intervention by government at any level in the United States into the operations of electric utilities that the government itself did not own.

Carter and PURPA Power

In 1977, at the urging of President Jimmy Carter, who liked to address the American public on television clad in a sweater to demonstrate his commitment to conservation, Congress created the Department of Energy. The new agency pulled together all of the federal energy-related activities that had previously been spread among countless entities, and major new activities were staffed for the first time: energy emergency planning and efforts to promote conservation and the use of renewable resources available in the United States. The FPC was replaced by the Federal Energy Regulatory Commission (FERC) which, though still an independent agency, was made part of the Department of Energy. By this action, the president and Congress intended to make clear that the federal policy toward electric and natural gas utilities would now include significant regulatory control by a prominent agency freed from the FPC's legacy of ineffectiveness and leniency.

With the country still running scared in the aftermath of the embargo, Carter was convinced that energy conservation must become a keystone of American economic and energy policies. The product of his concern was another piece of legislation, this one constituting a historic break with Insull's innovations.

The Public Utility Regulatory Policies Act of 1978,[14] known simply as PURPA, marked the beginning of the end of the idea that electric utilities were "natural monopolies." The regulatory bargain that had given utilities exclusive service territories in return for their acceptance of rate-setting by government regulators was in effect canceled, or at least modified.

The new law was driven by the simple notion that government had to give incentives to the electric industry to get it to rely on domestic, renewable, or efficient resources and substantially reduce its reliance on expensive and vulnerable imports. To accomplish this objective, the traditional utility itself would be bypassed. In the process, Congress managed to shift regulatory authority vested in the states to the federal level.

By requiring utilities to obtain from third parties some of the power they supplied to customers, PURPA represented the beginning of the end of the vertically integrated or bundled utility, which had owned the generator, the meter on the customer's house, and everything in between. The utilities had become dependent on fossil-fueled generators, but now the government would require them to purchase from companies using renewable resources or more efficient methods of producing power.

The principal new players in the electric business were known as "small power producers," because utilities were required only to purchase from units that were generally much smaller than their traditional resources. By keeping the units small, policy-makers intended that they could get into service quickly, because gaining environmental clearances and the necessary investment would be easier for them. They would also have only a gradual impact on the utility supply mix. The idea was to move as rapidly as possible away from imported fuel. The small power producers were required to derive their generation from renewable fuels like water, wind, and solar. Not surprisingly, some of the earliest units were tiny hydro facilities built where electricity had first been generated decades earlier. In fact, most of the initial spate of small power production came from extracting the energy from water going over existing dams.

The other new players were cogenerators, which would use fuel combustion to serve two different uses. A cogenerator could use steam both to produce electricity and for industrial processes. For example, a paper mill could use steam first to generate electricity and then reuse it in paper production. It would sell the power to the utility if the power company paid it more than the mill's cost of electricity, an approach possible under PURPA. Of course, it could use the power itself and reduce its purchases from the utility. Because cogeneration was deemed to promote efficient energy use, it was included under PURPA. Small power producers relying on renewables and cogenerators were known as qualifying facilities (QFs), because they qualified for the required purchase by utilities.

Utilities vigorously opposed the mandated power purchase because of the threat to their monopoly. They argued that they alone had the business knowledge and experience not available to the new players. But they failed to convince Carter and the Democratic Congress to back away from PURPA, because American dependence on foreign fuel supplies had continued to mount and the memory of the embargo had not yet faded.

PURPA got another boost when Congress passed the Fuel Use

Act,[15] banning any additional use of natural gas by utilities to generate electricity. The Carter administration believed that natural gas was running out and it should not be use for new, large-scale purposes. At the same time, the new law did not ban the use of natural gas by QFs, enabling them to avoid higher oil prices. This law, not repealed until 1987, gave added impetus to the use of renewables.

The National Energy Conservation Policy Act,[16] also signed into law in 1978 as part of the National Energy Act[17] package of laws, required utilities to provide electricity conservation services as well as the power itself. This measure was similar to asking tobacco companies to advertise against smoking, and the utilities were unenthusiastic. Yet another new law in the package promoted both cogeneration and solar and wind power through a tax credit that would go beyond the existing investment tax credit.

The objective of Carter's legislation may have been to get "off oil" but it also got the country off of its complete dependence on utilities. The utilities had long used a cartoon character known as Reddy Kilowatt to promote the use of electricity and thus enhance their profits. Reddy even urged people to purchase new and bigger electric appliances. Now the utilities had to abandon their old friend and exile him to a world from which he was not supposed to return ever again.

The biggest boost to PURPA came again from the Middle East. PURPA was signed on November 9, 1978. On January 16, 1979, the shah of Iran was forced to flee his country. Under the shah, Iran had amassed great wealth, thanks mainly to the run-up in oil prices resulting from the embargo, but the shah had become increasingly autocratic, and Iranian militants and Shia religious leadership wanted him replaced. With his departure and the return of Ayatollah Khomeini from exile, the Shia triumphed.

The Iranian revolution evoked the aura of the 1973 crisis, and oil prices again spiked sharply. Prices had eased somewhat after the embargo, but the 1979 increase, caused mostly by fear and uncertainty, sent crude oil prices from $13 a barrel to more than $23. Iranian oil fields shut down, reducing supplies for a few months but causing far less of a shortage than had occurred during the embargo. Still, lines again formed at gas stations. If a message were needed to remind Washington about the country's energy vulnerability, Iran provided it. PURPA and the other elements of the National Energy Policy seemed like a very good idea.

Avoided Cost and PURPA'S Decline

Theoretically, PURPA should have cost customers nothing. They were expected to pay no more for qualifying "PURPA power" than they would have otherwise had to pay. The cost of PURPA power should have been no greater than the cost of non-PURPA power that the utility had avoided. The price of PURPA was called "avoided cost." For the first time, the price of purchased power would be determined not by the seller's cost of production but by the purchasers' costs. If it cost a utility 5 cents a kilowatt-hour to generate power, it could pay a QF that amount without regard to what the QF's actual cost might be. It would take a U.S. Supreme Court decision to confirm that this new approach did not amount to seizing any of the utility's unused generators without compensation.[18] But the Court said that the utility could continue to recover from customers those costs that could not be avoided, such as debt service payments on generators, and even its authorized profit. Despite the theory that PURPA's effect on customers should be invisible, the Court's ruling made it virtually certain that the price of power would increase if the utility could recover unavoidable costs of unused generators plus the full cost of the replacement power.

The avoided-cost provision of the law left an opening for the utilities. The determination of what costs the utility would "avoid" was open to discussion and possibly litigation. The power companies believed that their larger units produced economies of scale that could not be matched by many small power producers. If the utilities had their way, the price of PURPA power from QFs might often turn out to be much higher than a low avoided cost, and the utilities would not be required to buy it.

Avoided cost became the battleground of the 1980s as PURPA began to be implemented. Congress left the determination of this cost to each state regulatory commission, virtually guaranteeing that there would be a patchwork of prices and policies across the country. The tax subsidies that the law included might bring down the cost of PURPA power, but it remained for the state regulators to create the market for such power by establishing the price to beat.

In some states, the crises of 1973 to 1974 and 1979 to 1980 had convinced regulators that electricity customers were vulnerable. Encouraged by environmentalists who worried about air emissions from oil-fired units, regulators in these states looked for ways to set avoided cost high enough to allow PURPA power to enter the market easily. It all depended on the forecasts of experts, and state regulators could hire from an array of firms that had made their reputations based on their patented forecasts. If state regulators wanted to encourage PURPA power, all they had to do was to sign up an expert to tell them that the price of oil would soon reach $50 a barrel and stay there. In states where regulators pursued these approaches, especially in California and the Northeast, plenty of QFs appeared. In fact, more QFs appeared than demand required.

From the customer's viewpoint, this policy had a fatal flaw. The customer cared less about underlying causes—wars in the Middle East or regime change in Iran—than about the soaring price of electricity, driven upward by the now-familiar fuel adjustment clause. Although many also found the notion of energy independence attractive, few understood that it could be attempted, much less achieved, only if they paid a price. When regulators set the price of oil high as a benchmark for PURPA suppliers, this meant that otherwise uneconomic generators could be built and a few developers could pocket a handsome profit. But rates would have to be increased immediately on the promise that the higher cost, locked in from the start, would be offset by savings later when the price of oil went above $50 a barrel. In such cases, either because they disliked utilities or because they were running scared that prices would reach astronomical levels, regulators imposed a heavy new tax on customers.

Elsewhere in the country, especially in the South, the reverse happened. Utilities brought greater pressure on regulators to set avoided cost low. Their effort was made easier in regions that were less dependent on oil—because they used coal, for instance—or where some part of the regional supply originated in federal power administrations. Occasionally, the key role was played by elected regulators, who were far less willing to pass on the costly implications of a policy designed to encourage renewables. They did not turn to experts who would provide frightening long-term forecasts of oil prices but looked only at current costs of power. The cumulative effect was to set avoided cost so low that no QFs would be possible. This policy pleased both the utilities by protecting their monopolies and their customers by protecting their rates. In effect, in states where avoided cost was set based on low estimates of capital costs and the current cost of fuel, regulators could undermine the National Energy Policy and gladly did so.

The 1980s found the country divided, with more than half the states doing little or nothing to abandon business as usual, while others, especially those in states where rates were high, moved to encourage new generators. In some states, more aggressive policies meant that utilities were required to buy from independent power producers even if those producers were not QFs.

Eventually, in the face of growing public discontent with state-set electricity rates, the policy of arbitrarily setting the price of PURPA power at a high avoided cost began to be abandoned by state regulators. Instead of regulators fixing the price, QFs would be asked to bid to meet the market's requirements, and the low bids would be selected. The first QFs had received the highest possible avoided costs, leaving far lower and less attractive rates for new arrivals. The PURPA supply began to dry up, but not until much damage had been done to customers. While this change was taking place at the state level, FERC, now a more effective and neutral regulator, began to consider whether cost-based rates for interstate electricity sales still made sense, with some supply now coming from generators that were being paid based not on their own costs but on the hypothetical costs of others.

Once PURPA had been enacted, Congress again had the taste for legislating about electric utilities. During the 1980s, it imposed tougher environmental controls on hydro projects, making it less likely that water power would make any new contribution to meeting renewable energy requirements. In practice, this new authority would lead to FERC ordering existing dams to be removed, actually reducing the amount of power from this historic renewable resource. But it enhanced the need for new generators.

Congress also provided tax incentives for the construction of new generators, whether by utilities or QFs. Owners of generating plants could speed up the normally allowed rate of depreciation on their tax returns. In the past, if a plant was depreciated over a twenty-five-year period, the owner would be allowed to count one-twenty-fifth of the cost as an expense in each year. But the new tax laws allowed the utility to deduct the entire cost from taxes in ten years or less even if the companies were writing off the costs over a far longer period, so that the owner would gain greater profits and presumably be encouraged by that to make larger investments. Even better, state regulators chose to act as if the utilities had not received the credit but had paid the higher taxes that would have resulted from the application of the normal depreciation rules. That way the utilities could collect from customers the revenues necessary to pay taxes higher than those they had actually paid.

The large utilities surveyed the scene at the end of the 1980s. PURPA had brought major changes in the way business was done in only a few states. In most of them, its effect was to increase rates unnecessarily as it became evident that the price of imported oil was not rising as expected. The slowing of price increases resulted from a growing awareness in the producing countries that they had become dependent on revenues from the major consuming countries. In addition, conservation had produced some effect, as new homes and old water heaters were better insulated. Finally, alternate fuels, mainly natural gas—which, after the 1978 legislation freeing the price of natural gas from federal price regulation, was found to be more plentiful than forecast—had begun to displace imported oil.

After the second energy crisis, the utilities found themselves in much better financial condition than they had expected. The Dow Utility Index had risen from about 100 in 1980 to more than 200 ten years later (and to 390 in 2005). The utility companies concluded that PURPA's effect in ending their monopoly might be turned to their advantage. Independent generation was obviously here to stay, and the utilities wanted to increase their initial efforts at diversification. They decided to launch an effort to convince Congress to let them own generators from which they could sell power to any utility just like the independent power producers.

PURPA and EPAct Get Technical

Aggregator: An entity that combines customers into power purchasing groups.

All requirements: The full electric service often required by municipal utilities, including power supply, transmission, and ancillary services. A marketer may assemble such a package for sale.

Ancillary services: Dispatch services and various kind of reserves need to accompany power supply from generators before delivery to the customer. They supplement transmission service.

Avoided cost: The price that could be paid to **QFs** for their power, equal to the cost of the traditional power supply that was not used.

Cogeneration: The use of a single-fuel consuming process to produce energy for two uses, for example, electricity and heating.

Congestion: The inability to transfer power from one area to another because of a lack of sufficient transmission lines. Congestion pricing allows affected entities to purchase power in the delivery area for use there to replace power from the supply area made inaccessible by inadequate transmission.

Cost of service: All of the allowed costs that a utility may recover from its customers. Based on the expected sales, a regulator divides this cost by the number of units of sales to derive the rate. This cost includes the rate of return.

Gross market: After restructuring, the trading of all power supply in an open-bid, competitive market. Contrast with **net market.**

Marketer: An entity that sells power. Usually owns some generators and purchases power from generators.

Net market: The trading of a relatively small amount of power supply in the open-bid competitive market with most power bought and sold in direct bilateral deals between two parties. Contrast with **gross market.**

Qualifying facility (QF): A generator that meets the requirements of

PURPA (renewable fuel, cogeneration) for required purchase by utilities. Requirement was eliminated by 2005 EPAct.

Rate of return: The profit margin that regulators allow utilities to add to other operating costs. Does not apply to unregulated entities.

Real-time: Also known as time-of-use or time-of-day, it tracks the cost of energy continuously so that customers can be charged according to the current cost.

Stranded cost: The investment in generation made by a utility that cannot be recovered because the generator has not been used because of the effect of PURPA or the 1992 EPAct.

4

REDDY'S RETURN: COMPETITION

W ashington gave the utilities what they wanted—a chance to compete in an unregulated market just as had been given to the PURPA generators. Congress created the conditions needed for an electricity market, which would make buyers and sellers free to make their own deals at unregulated prices. That could mean the end of the utility monopoly, because utilities would be allowed to sell power in the traditional service areas of other utilities. The companies could count themselves lucky that there was both a supportive Republican president and a susceptible Democratic Congress. The Democrats included some who were impressed by the possibilities that PURPA had created for unregulated players, known as nonutility generators (NUGs) to sell power to utilities and others from states, especially in the South, where it made political sense to be responsive to the power companies.

Congress came up with legislation both to grant the utilities greater freedom from the strictures of PUHCA and to limit their ability to exploit their monopoly position. The result was the Energy Policy Act of 1992, quickly dubbed EPAct.[19] This law caused as radical a transformation of the business as had PUHCA in 1935 and changed the face of utility industry. It ended regulation of generators in the wholesale electric business and opened access to transmission lines for players other than the owners of those lines. It introduced the operation of the free market into the electric business on the promise of the fundamental tenet of the free-market system: competition will produce lower costs for customers.

By separating generation from the rest of the utility business, the law recognized that making power was not truly a monopoly utility business. Electricity customers had always been required to pay the costs of all utility generating plants, even those that worked either poorly or not at all. FERC had begun to allow independent generators to set their own, unregulated prices, because these suppliers would have to beat regulated utility prices. EPAct went further and shifted the burden of risk for making bad decisions about generation from utility ratepayers to investors in independent generation. The relief to customers could be considerable. That transfer of risk responsibility, far more than prices resulting from competition, would turn out to be the greatest benefit of restructuring.

Without realizing what they had done when they enacted PURPA, President Carter and the Democratic Congress had in 1978 introduced competition into a business long believed to be in the hands of natural monopolies. If it succeeded in no other way, PURPA proved that generators owned by companies not otherwise involved in the utility business were able to provide reliable power supply to serve customers. The utilities had reluctantly acquiesced in the adoption of PURPA because of the national need for decisive action to control reliance on foreign oil and their recognition that even with PURPA, utility generation would continue to dominate. But PURPA's success, however limited, made EPAct inevitable.

EPAct: The Rules Change

EPAct is an insider's law, a product of the utilities and independent generators. They gained political support for EPAct among those who were convinced that it would guarantee lower prices for consumers. Without any careful analysis of where the new law might lead, President G.H.W. Bush and Congress seemed to think it could do no harm and might provide real benefit to customers. Part of the Reagan Revolution that had swept the country was the belief that the private sector could do much of what government had done—and better. Even a Democratic Congress could no longer resist the lure of the free market.

The law had been inspired by two previous landmark regulatory developments, both showing signs of producing the lower prices that supposedly came from competition. The first was the restructuring of the natural gas industry, a sector over which FERC had broader powers under the Natural Gas Act[20] than it had for electricity under the Federal Power Act. FERC decided that pipeline

Customers—Wholesale and Retail (in millions) 2003		
Investor-owned Utilities	92.77	68.9%
Publicly owned Utilities	19.50	14.5%
Cooperatives (wholesale/retail)	16.16	12.0%
Power Marketers	6.08	4.5%
Federal Power Agencies	0.04	0.0%
	134.55	

Source: American Public Power Association

companies should no longer own the gas they transported, making them into common carriers. In sharp contrast, electric industry restructuring under the new law left most of the utilities intact, so they could own the electricity and all of the facilities from the generator to the meter at a customer's home.

Complicating the comparison was the mistaken belief that electricity is a commodity like natural gas. Unlike natural gas and other products traded in organized markets, which can be stored for later use, electricity has to be consumed at the time it is produced. Only small amounts of water for hydro generation can be kept behind dams, creating lakes known as impoundments that can be drawn down later. Tiny amounts—relative to the size of the market—can also be pumped up into elevated storage reservoirs at night to flow down during the day to produce power. Power cannot be efficiently stored and then released to lower electricity prices.

The other major change inspiring the changes in the electric industry was the massive transformation of the telephone industry. Telephone customers can choose among a variety of long-distance companies that actively bid for their patronage. But just about the only thing that the power business and the telephone business have in common is wires. And even the wires are different. To save costs, power lines carrying electric current are usually bare, not insulated, and vulnerable to interruption, while insulated telephone lines, protected to avoid static, carry only small amounts of current and are more reliable. More important, of course, is the lack of any telephonic equivalent of the costly generator. The telephone industry could be restructured simply by changing rights with respect to the use of existing lines and switches. While FERC could do the same for power lines, there also have to be enough generators available to serve customers at the ends of those lines. From the start of the electric industry restructuring, the hopes of those looking for a major change for residential customers, as had happened for telephone service, were doomed to be disappointed.

In addition, changes in the telephone industry went right down to the retail customers, but in the electric sector, FERC was limited to interstate transmission and wholesale relationships between supplying companies and those companies who served end users. Congress knew it would encounter a flood of opposition from the states and utilities if it attempted to require open transmission access to filter down to the state-regulated retail level. The power companies were content to get a law that would deal with wholesale transactions, while the retail option remained only theoretically available on a state-by-state basis. Some companies that did not want to open themselves to retail competition were confident that they could resist it in states where they operated.

Separating Generation and Transmission

FERC wanted to make sure that owners of both generators and transmission lines could not favor themselves over others in the use of those lines. Power companies would have to take clear steps to keep their unregulated generating business separate from their regulated utility business. A single company owning both generating plants and transmission lines would have to create a holding company, and here the power companies ran directly into PUHCA prohibitions. The utilities wanted both to own independent generation and to exercise a monopoly right to serve their traditional customers. The potential for self-dealing, a target of the 1935 law, was great.

The solution in EPAct was the creation of a new class of generators known as Exempt Wholesale Generators (EWGs)—exempt, that is, from PUHCA prohibitions against owning companies in other states in the absence of a registered holding company and against self-dealing.

A utility can own generators through separate corporate entities anywhere in the United States without running afoul of the 1935 law. But EWGs must provide information to states to insure that their power supply will be reliable based both on their technical competence and their access to financial backing. The SEC was given added authority by EPAct to control investment by holding companies in EWGs and to protect American ratepayers from any losses on the companies' overseas investments. Even with these restrictions, utilities and independent power producers were satisfied that their lobbying efforts would get them into the unregulated end of the business.

While this change in the law solved the utilities' problem, they had to pay a price for this newly acquired ability to participate in an open generation market. The door had to be opened to other generators to enter the utility owner's market to serve the utility itself and any wholesale customers. EPAct undertook the revolutionary step of requiring that the transmission system become the equivalent of a common carrier. The local utility would continue to have a monopoly right to serve its own end-use customers, but behind the scenes, there would be wholesale competition.

FERC found that the law required some additional rules to insure that the transmission lines would be operated fairly for all comers. Without detailed rules, transmission owners could try to impose on all new users of the power lines seemingly neutral qualifications that would in fact have the effect of discriminating in favor of the existing user—the owner itself.

But change did not come easily. The first roadblock to reform was the demand by the utilities, which now risked losing wholesale customers, that they be compensated for the loss of business. They argued that they had built generators in the belief that their wholesale customers were locked in and that if those customers were now allowed to purchase power from others, the traditional host utilities would have to be compensated for their unused investment. This compensation became known as "stranded-cost" recovery. The consumer would have to pay for the cost of the competitive power supply plus stranded costs. The net price to the consumer might be the same or even higher than it had been before open access, thus killing competition.

But FERC let the old-line utilities down. In a pre-EPAct, New Hampshire case, a utility argued that the "public interest" entitled it to stranded cost. In a Maine case, a utility argued that when it had agreed to a contract that banned stranded costs, it had not expected competition. In both cases, FERC sided with the wholesale customer, saying that stranded cost could be charged only when it was authorized by the contract. However, FERC policy would increasingly allow stranded cost, which would be a factor slowing the promise of change in the electric industry.

The landmark FERC order—somewhat whimsically numbered Order 888 after the new address of the FERC offices at 888 First Street in Northeast Washington—laid down the requirements imposed on transmission owners. They would have to have a separate schedule of rates for use of the transmission system; in the past, such rates had always been "bundled" into their total costs. A potential customer could then know what the cost of using the wires would be. FERC also required that a management barrier—a "Chinese wall"—had to be erected between employees handing generation and those handling wires, so that the utility would not be able quietly to favor its own generation in serving its wholesale customers. Despite the required and much acclaimed codes of conduct for utility employees, it was easy to be skeptical about just how independent the transmission managers were likely to be.

Order 888 went on to lay out hundreds of pages of rules that would be necessary to insure that customers would be treated fairly.

This order took the bare bones of wholesale access mandated by EPAct and made them into a thorough and comprehensive body of rules that would cause the desired change in the power industry. It made clear the promise of EPAct: if utilities wanted transmission access to the markets of others, they would have to provide such access themselves.

However, Order 888 would still have to undergo a trial by fire in the federal courts as states and utilities challenged FERC's right to adopt such sweeping rules. For example, the federal commission said that it had the right to force utilities to set a transmission rate even for their own service to their customers so that it could be sure that wholesale users were paying the same amount for transmission as did captive retail customers. Challenged by states that believed this provision to be an invasion of their regulatory prerogatives, FERC needed a decision of the U.S. Supreme Court to confirm that right on the basis of EPAct.[21]

Opposition to Order 888 by the major transmission owners, some of the same companies that had called for the kind of open access enjoyed by the PURPA suppliers, suggested that they had not fully considered the implications of their desire to sell generation just as PURPA suppliers did—in wanting to obtain the benefits of selling power to others, they had not understood or accepted how they would have to open themselves to competition. Many state regulators also saw more change than they had expected, as regulatory power shifted from the states to the federal government. Industry restructuring was going to be a battle.

FERC Mandates Markets

FERC concluded that merely mandating an open-access grid, so that suppliers would have a ready and uncontested opportunity to serve wholesale customers, would not be enough to assure that the market would be competitive. The commission decided that it would have to develop the market itself. There had never been a large or sophisticated market for electricity. The logical outgrowth of the decision to open the transmission system, FERC reasoned, was the need to make sure that access was used to support a market and that the market had some rules.

FERC also concluded that emerging markets would have to be larger than the service area of a single utility, both to take advantage of the ease by which power could now pass across systems and to reduce the likelihood of domination of a small market by a single utility. For example, the six New England states, whose territory amounted to only one fiftieth of the United States and which had nine transmission owners, could be advantageously brought together by requiring the owners to merge the management of their systems. Still, questions remained about how far the policy of consolidation should go in other regions.

There are physical limits on the size of the market. Unlike commodities, electricity cannot be shipped over a thousand miles or more, because some of it is lost as it travels over the wires. It would be like a railcar of oranges with its door left partially open and losing an orange each mile it traveled. The shipper's cost of oranges delivered to its destination would be increased with every piece of fallen fruit. Because such losses occur in the electric business, there are physical limits on how far power may be transmitted at reasonable cost.

Of course, FERC was aware of this but also believed that if a larger market is created, the transmission of electricity between adjoining areas could have the same effect as actually creating a single, physical market. One might call this regulation by contagion.

FERC also insisted that transmission grids of groups of utilities should be under independent control, which came to be called

Independent System Operators (ISOs) or Regional Transmission Organizations (RTOs). Utilities were strongly encouraged to create such entities, which would then establish themselves independent of the utilities. While the utilities would continue to own their own transmission lines, they would no longer be able to control access to those lines. Despite the power companies' maintaining at least some control over transmission, ISOs were supposed to gain functional control, essentially a supervisory role, over the operation of the system. This split responsibility over transmission caused continuing problems. The ISOs had their own costs and rates, which filtered down to the customer. Supposedly the customer, to whom most of the industry changes and certainly all of the ISO developments were invisible, would find paying for an ISO to be a good deal, especially in return for the benefits of the competitive market and its potentially lower rates.

The complex market rules developed by FERC made it difficult for small players to afford the costs of compliance, improving the opportunities for larger players. FERC's policy of promoting large market areas also favored big companies with the resources necessary to participate in an expanded market. Besides the benefits of broader markets and weakened utility control, the federal regulators believed that if power could be traded over wider areas, the business would be more attractive for suppliers. The suppliers would face less uncertainty if they were not dependent on smaller, local markets. And prices over larger areas would tend to become homogenized, spreading the benefits of competition. Because of this, FERC pressed utilities to place their transmission systems under the control of independent system operators controlling as wide an area as possible. Although without the power to compel compliance, FERC nevertheless foresaw a country with as few as four to six system operators.

While it encountered resistance in New York, New England, the South, and the West—which were accustomed to their own regional arrangements—FERC fostered some large transmission arrangements. The extreme case was a linkage, announced in 2005, of three already large transmission groups. The Midwest ISO operates in fifteen states and one Canadian province. Linked to it is the PJM Interconnection (originally named for Pennsylvania, Jersey, Maryland), which operates in twelve states and the District of Columbia. The final link was the TVA, which provides power supply in seven states. Together, these three groups transmit or provide almost half the power supply in the eastern half of the United States. Closely coordinated, they could provide the basis for a new economic reality in the power business.

Because FERC wanted the transmission system managed by entities that had no interest in the generating end of the business, it considered going beyond ISOs to promote companies that would purchase the transmission facilities of the utilities and operate them independently. The new companies would be regulated utilities and would stand to profit from any increased use of their wires, making them natural advocates of the open market. Many players in the power market favored this policy because the operators' costs would be subject to traditional regulatory review and the new owners would have incentives to build new lines.

For a while, FERC itself seemed to favor this independent transmission initiative. A few companies were launched but met with only limited success. The utilities did not want to sell their transmission lines, which they often regarded as of great strategic value, and some obviously believed that the pressure to comply fully with FERC's strategy for carrying out Order 888 would gradually dissipate.

Companies planning to get into the transmission business during the period when FERC first showed its enthusiasm for independent ownership had been moderate in their proposals. TransElect, headed by veteran utility executives, and Atlantic Transco, backed by Wall Street investors, offered to make an acquisition without raising rates to customers, provided they could use a new capital structure—the relationship between debt and equity used to finance the purchase and future expansions. These capped rates would be guaranteed to the purchaser for a fixed period, so that if the independent transmission company (ITC) could operate more efficiently, they could retain the added profits. Customers would be protected from any increases. The ITC would compensate the former owner at the current value on which it was earning a return on investment plus the amount of any taxes for which the transaction might make the former owner liable. The former owner could, in effect, convert its investment in transmission into other needed facilities without additional cost to customers. Sometimes the ITCs even offered the owners a premium payment for making the transaction.

A few transmission sales did take place, especially where the selling utility had become a "wires company" after having divested itself of its generators. The purchaser usually acquired the transmission grid plus the local distribution lines, an attractive deal because distribution was increasingly seen as a profitable business. But few transactions took place in which a utility voluntarily sold its transmission lines. In the end, FERC backed off its support for ITCs and yielded to the strong opposition of utilities wielding great political power, like the Southern Company, a utility operating in four southern states.

ISOs, the independent operators, became the essential but costly and complicating factor in the development of the market. ISOs have no incentive to cut the costs of their operations and tend to become expensive utility bureaucracies. They might seek to act in what they would define as the best interests of the end users, but they let their preoccupation with tinkering with the market take priority over their concern for customers.

Just before the passage of the 2005 Energy Policy Act, National Grid, a British-based company that had acquired wires companies and aspired to own and operate transmission lines across the United States, issued a paper calling for a return to the policy of encouraging ITCs. It complained of "an outdated industry structure that does not encourage the incremental investment in transmission that National Grid believes would yield significant customer benefits."[22] It argued that transmission should be regarded as "a market commodity rather than a market enabler." Not surprisingly, and in line with the trend toward larger companies dominating the business, it insisted that independent transmission owners and operators needed to operate "over a wide area." While its arguments were sound, its obvious self-interest could only serve to undermine them.

In 2005, a new energy law would give only a little encouragement to those seeking incentives for new transmission investment. It promoted streamlined and simplified environmental reviews, consistent with the Bush administration's policy, going as far as to provide for transmission "corridors" in which FERC could force transmission. To accomplish this goal, FERC was given the same kind of eminent domain rights that could override local objections as it had long been authorized to use for natural gas pipelines. The law permitted higher investment returns to encourage more transmission but did not suggest that FERC should move transmission ownership from traditional utilities to new independent companies. While the higher net revenues might encourage the construction of new lines, the owners were almost certain to be the utilities themselves, not independent companies.

And then came the market rules. Most markets in the free-enterprise system develop organically. As they evolve, regulation becomes inevitable to insure that the market is not "gamed" by some participants undermining fair and open competition and to protect the consumer, who is supposed to benefit from the operation of the market. Perhaps the classic case began in the late eighteenth century when a group of men met on a street corner in New York to trade shares in companies doing business locally, creating the first American stock market. Over two centuries, this grew into a series of sophisticated markets for trading stocks, bonds, and a host of financial products through high-speed electronic operations. Along the way, federal and state laws and regulations were adopted to regulate the products and exchanges. But Congress and state legislatures did not dictate how the market would organize itself.

Not so for the electric market. The purpose of restructuring was to replace a system in which regulators set the prices of a monopoly product with one in which the arm's-length interaction between buyers and sellers would set the price for competitively supplied generation. Faced with a choice between allowing the market to grow by itself with regulatory oversight to insure that abuses were prevented, on the one hand, and regulating all aspects of the market, on the other, FERC chose to regulate everything. This decision, made in the traditional obscurity of utility regulation, out of public view, would be one of the principal causes of the failure of restructuring of the electric industry.

FERC rules treated electricity as a traded commodity rather than as a consumer product. While the regulators knew that electricity lacks one essential element of commodities—the ability to be stored—they believed they could develop a system that would allow for that factor. If the market were an extremely short one, with only a day between the time the price was set and the product was manufactured and delivered, perhaps it could work.

But they had no experience in establishing commodity markets.

Regulators had traditionally made judgments about whether monopoly owners could build facilities and charge customers for them and what costs could legitimately be passed on to customers. Virtually everything they did ended up as a decision about the rates that could properly be charged. Not knowing how to construct markets, FERC was also ignorant of how to protect consumers from unscrupulous market operators.

Problems arose because FERC insisted on a "one size fits all" approach. It tried to set the size of markets and define the products, all in the naïve belief that the customers would benefit. Its goal was a large, if not national, market with many participants vying for the business of millions of customers. But the market FERC designed was so complex that potential competitors were unable to master the rules and dropped out of the business, leaving only a relative handful of sellers. Because of its lack of knowledge and experience and its incorrect forecasts about how the market would develop, FERC failed to produce positive results but succeeded in creating more costs and complications.

The complexity of what FERC created could be measured by the sheer weight of the documents. Order 888 needed to be supplemented by Order 888A and then Order 2000 and then 2000A. Taken together, these basic documents ran to thousands of pages. And then there was the myriad of pages of market rules and transmission tariffs that FERC required of ISOs and similar bodies. Any prospective player would have to devote millions of dollars merely to get to the starting line of the new electric market. And if the incumbent utilities, especially the transmission owners, wanted to hamper industry restructuring, the complexity of the rules made it easy for them to string out their responses to requests for transmission access from generators. At some point, generators and resellers of their power—the marketers—would quit from sheer despair. Yet, even as the market became populated by only a handful of marketers, FERC failed to adjust its policies.

The SMD Fiasco

One of the most classic of FERC's fumbles was its effort to mandate what it called Standard Market Design (SMD). It wanted all power markets in the United States to operate under a single set of rules in the belief that if suppliers faced the same rules across the country, they would find it easier to operate anywhere. Of course, a single system would also be easier to regulate. The SMD proposal went along with the FERC plan to create the largest possible markets.

But SMD ran into a storm of opposition. States in the South and West, where large power systems had traditionally operated without tight regional arrangements, vociferously opposed the imposition of a regulatory system totally at odds with their normal practices. They claimed that FERC had never been given the authority to mandate a national market design. Rep. Brian Baird, one of Washington State's congressional representatives, attacked "the top-down, cookie cutter approach that FERC is trying to impose."[23] States opposing SMD were in harmony with, if not actually prompted by, their incumbent utilities. These power companies wanted to do business as they always had and felt they could better resist FERC changes if there were no new market design that might open their territories to service by others. Finally, even if SMD were to be adopted, it might require years of negotiating to take into account the complex collection of special practices that had grown up all across the country. Only marketers, who saw their path to customers eased by a standard design, supported SMD. But SMD engendered so much opposition that it died of its own weight.

An inevitable result of creating a market by combining smaller existing markets is that the new arrangement is likely to homogenize prices so that they become close to the average of the prices that had prevailed in the smaller units. A broad market with a uniform price expands the scope and flexibility of action by the marketers. But those whose prices would increase because of the new market are almost certain to oppose it. FERC's SMD effort overlooked the opposition of states in the Northwest and Southeast, which had access to a regional market containing large federal power resources and feared that a national market would result in their subsidizing the Northeast and Midwest. While there might be some poetic justice to those taxpayers who contributed heavily to the support of the federal power administrations getting something back on their investment, the opposition showed that the FERC proposal was politically unrealistic.

The many state responses to SMD explain, in part, why FERC had proposed it. Some states and utilities flatly opposed restructuring and had no market design and no market. Others pushed extreme solutions that, as we shall see in the case of California, could not work in practice. Many states tried to regulate, cap, or mandate retail rates while the cost of supply was not regulated. Some considered setting retail prices high enough to encourage competition. If SMD was an idea that could not happen, almost all state plans contained the seeds of their own destruction. What everybody wanted to do, it seemed, was to dictate the market system, not to let it evolve, perhaps slowly and under sufficient scrutiny to avoid anticompetitive practices—no matter that most of the American economy works that way.

By freeing generation from utility regulation altogether, the new policy created yet another problem. Previously it had been possible for system operators to require that utility-owned generators either be located where they would not unduly strain the transmission grid or pay to upgrade the system. Sometimes, the utilities themselves might pay for transmission upgrades to handle new generators, if the modifications improved reliability and had little or no impact on rates. One way to maintain the reliability of the grid and keep transmission costs under control was to require that a generator be sited near the customers it was supposed to serve. In the new, competitive world, generators could be located wherever it was the easiest to obtain the approval of environmental regulators. That meant that new generation could be located in rural areas, far from the main concentration of customers to be served. The result of these uncoordinated siting decisions was that the existing transmission lines from the generators' locations to their markets turned out to be inadequate.

To deal with this unanticipated situation, regulators came up with a plan that would supposedly slow the need to provide new transmission facilities. It was called "congestion pricing," based on the idea of charging higher tolls on certain roads at times of peak traffic conditions. At times when it is impossible for power to flow from one part of the system to another, customer load is supplied from local generators at prices higher than if the customers had obtained electricity from more remote and inaccessible but less expensive generators. The theory is that as the frequency of congestion pricing increases, it will finally become less expensive to construct new transmission lines to provide uninterrupted access to the lower-cost generation.

Forcing People to Pay

Over time, regulators arrived at an even worse solution. Congestion pricing became a way of encouraging generation companies to site their facilities as close to their customers as possible. Presumably they would want to avoid this pricing system and, if so, they would reduce the need for more transmission lines. When that theory proved not to work as well as expected, FERC decided that ISOs could set unusually high market prices for the output of generators in high density areas that are difficult to access. The policy was called Locational Installed Capacity (LICAP) or Reliability Pricing Model (RPM). Presumably, the high guaranteed prices would attract more generators to a congested market area—but the artificially high generating costs would be imposed on customers. The new, competitive world would look remarkably like the old, regulated world, where a regulatory authority could impose uneconomic generating costs on customers. If regulators forced customers to subsidize competition, then where were the benefits of restructuring? With all that was going wrong in the electric industry from the consumer's perspective, LICAP offered the possibility of even worse effects.

The outcry against this policy was loud and angry. New England's states and regulators protested, but a FERC administrative judge dismissed their appeal without a hearing, calling it "flawed and inflamed."[24] New England fury at this judge's decision was so strong that a provision was added to the 2005 energy law dealing with the New England situation and calling on FERC to "carefully consider the States' objections." Obviously, restructuring was not working well.

Much the same battle developed in the PJM market, which extends from New Jersey to Illinois. In 2005, ComEd, the Exelon subsidiary serving the Chicago area, proposed a 37 percent rate increase, including 17 percent for capacity payments under the RPM. The RPM money would go to the utility because it is a generation owner, although it would not be required to invest in new generators. The consultant for the Illinois Citizens Utility Board (CUB) said the payment would amount to a "huge wealth transfer from ratepayers to owners of existing generation."[25] Illinois CUB executive David Kotala said that "Exelon alone stands to reap windfall revenues of as much as $1.2 billion under this self-serving plan."

Regulators were eager to replace their control over the industry with "market-based" measures and based their support for LICAP on their own forecasts of how the market would work, not on actual data. John Anderson, the longtime president of the trade group representing the largest industrial electricity customers, said of these forecasts, which regulators presented as market-related studies: "They're constructs of regulators who draw demand curves and price schedules based on their guesses about the future."[26] He argued vigorously that customers would simply end up paying for generators without any assurance that there would be new supplies.

The LICAP debate symbolized the degree to which a policy to insure and promote transmission access had been diverted into dealing with the absence of such access by promoting generators. In part, this diversion was driven by worries that there would not be enough power supply to meet the general public's and industry's insatiable appetite for electricity. The system operators concluded that by promoting generation in the proper location—near the customers—it would be possible to feed that appetite while avoiding transmission bottlenecks. In fact the policy delayed the addition of new transmission, further raising the likelihood of enriching generators at the expense of end-use customers.

Industry restructuring was based on the belief that if you allow anybody to generate and have transmission access, "they will come." In fact, at first generators did come, offering plans for new plants well in excess of need in some areas. But reckless enthusiasm for the generating business brought business failures and a subsequent reluctance to propose new generation. The market, unlike a regulated utility, had no central (and regulated) plan for meeting customer needs. With business failures, generation investors became increasingly risk-averse. Generation capacity was not being built. Enter LICAP/RPM, with its potential for profligate spending of customer money.

What happened to the underlying principle that there would be open transmission access and that FERC would require more lines to be constructed if there were a demonstrated need for them? Although transmission is less costly and less of a business risk than generation, states and regulators have been reluctant to spend any money to encourage construction of new lines. In New England, southwest Connecticut needed improved connection with the rest of the region and beyond, but other New England states were reluctant to have their customers pay for upgrades to the grid when most of the benefit would go to Connecticut. Because of this regional refusal to support a transmission upgrade, it was, perhaps, not surprising that ISO-New England would then turn to LICAP and more generation.

The industry adjusted to EPAct and began to thrive. The big companies, once threatened by competition, survived and now dominate the market. The transmission business turned out to be such a good source of income that utilities are loath to part with it. Generators have begun to look forward to big, mandated payoffs. Even at the state level, the distribution business, which had seemed so unattractive, became a solid moneymaker as more transactions went across existing lines at no added cost.

The passage of EPAct had embodied the promise of a new competitive world: regulation would cede much of its price-setting authority to the market, and consumers would see the benefits in the form of lower electricity costs.

But the promise went mostly unfulfilled. Government set the table not for a new, competitive world but for a series of catastrophic and dangerous problems that would expose customers to risk paralleled only by the later days of Samuel Insull. Consumers soon found that competition often meant higher electric rates without any improvement in reliability.

States Go Their Own Way

The framers of EPAct had carefully refrained from requiring open access to the grid for retail customers—the residential, commercial, and industrial customers that consume electricity. The states would certainly have gone to great lengths to kill a bill that would so obviously have intervened in matters traditionally reserved to regulation by them. It was left up to each state to decide if it would allow retail competition, with customers allowed to purchase power in the open market instead of through their local utility. But FERC said that if a state adopted retail access, it would have to follow the federal open-access and market rules.

In most states, nothing happened. Utilities accustomed to captive markets were reluctant to give them up. States whose governments were friendly to the utilities opted not to allow retail competition. States in the South and West, most of which had long been accustomed to reliance on low-cost supplies from federal power administrations, did not want to loosen their grasp on a good deal by giving competition a try. The subsidized price of federal power made private investment in competitive generation unattractive, so states from Alaska to Florida remained mostly unaffected by electric industry restructuring.

Though the new market led to the creation of new players—independent generators and power marketers—they did not bring the promised results of industry restructuring to customers. As we shall see, these new players would be absorbed by old utilities. Restructuring could not change the underlying physical and demographic realities: existing generators, power lines designed to serve a regulated market, customers either uninterested or exploited. The utilities were not, for the most part, ready for the kind of competition that was being offered to them—and at times being forced on them.

Those states that decided retail customers should have access to the market, such as New England, the Mid-Atlantic states, New York, and California, started the process in the belief that residential customers would experience the same kind of competitive rush as when telephone services had been opened up to competition. The phone would virtually ring off the wall with offers when retail access occurred; the presence of many competitors coupled with lower prices would make the new version of the electric industry a great success.

Unfortunately, the competitive revolution fizzled. Electricity is actually a far more complex package of services than telephone service, which has no functional equivalent of generators. To put together a package equally as marketable as telephone service, a company would have to assemble the generator, transmission access, and backup power. Because nobody was ready to invest in these costly elements for a multifaceted generating package to support speculative sales, electricity customers' phones remained silent.

The apparent reason for industry restructuring, especially at the retail level, was to introduce competition that would lead to lower prices for customers. In only a few states were proponents careful to say that they were merely promising the opportunity for the market rather than the regulators to set the price of electric power, whatever the result. In other states, to insure that the promise of competition would be realized immediately, legislatures imposed ceilings or caps on electric rates, occasionally even setting them below the current regulated price. Such legislative policies reflected faith in the results of competition without any apparent understanding of the underlying economics of the electricity business, but they made restructuring the politically popular thing to do.

The lure of competition was especially strong in states with high rates. By the turn of the new century, almost half the states, principally in the Northeast and California, had moved to open their retail markets to competition. A major driving force behind this move was the fact that utilities in some of these states had built costly and poorly designed generators and had passed the bills for their mistakes on to their customers. In the future, at least, customers could be protected from the burden of useless generator costs. The story of the Washington Public Power Supply System (WPPSS) was legendary. It had set out to build five nuclear power plants but succeeded in completing only one of them. While it got out from under most of the costs, its customers were forced to come up with $753 million to pay off bondholders, in return for which they received nothing—not a single kilowatt-hour. Not surprisingly, WPPSS came to be known as "Whoops," and the embarrassment finally forced it to change its name. Competition was supposed to protect customers from another Whoops.

The new state regimes varied widely. In a much-heralded plan in Pennsylvania, customers could choose between regulated utility generation and unregulated independent sources, with the host utility required to transmit the power from either source. In Maine, the utilities were forced by law to sell their generators. Customers there could choose from independent suppliers that made offers to them, and power that was purchased competitively on their behalf if they took no action. In these states, customers could choose to enter into long- or short-term arrangements that best suited their needs. California was far more aggressive and not only regulated the market but also regulated the customers by determining the permissible length of their power supply arrangements.

Market design by state regulators was often a case of the uninformed controlling the unknown to the detriment of the unfortunate. As soon as restructuring was approved in a state, the regulators would chase off in hot pursuit of a market scheme that would be most likely to transmit the proper market prices to customers. California simply banned long-term power transactions, the traditional backbone of the market. Not only did it decree that the utilities would have to buy power at market prices on a daily basis, but the state also decided that the utilities could charge their customers only what the regulators allowed even if that were below the market price. Caught in this price squeeze, California utilities would ultimately plunge into bankruptcy, pushed over the edge by state regulation.

This rigid, short-term policy did not always suit the customer's interests. For example, a resort hotel that wants to set prices for conventions several years in the future would benefit from knowing its long-term power costs so that it can offer guaranteed prices for future reservations. If it must accept short-term power prices, it will either have to take more risk in quoting its own prices or pass the risk on to others in the form of higher charges.

Under restructuring, the very nature of the market itself became an issue. Traditionally, a utility would enter into long-term power supply arrangements to serve the complete requirements of its customers. It would own or line up generation under so-called bilateral contracts directly linking the buyer and the seller. It might need to buy a small amount of power on a short-term basis. One kind of short-term service is called "load following," which means that a generator is available to crank its output up or down from one second to another as needed. Under bilateral deals, all of the power supply was put in place for an extended period. FERC wanted to see changes in this kind of arrangement.

In theory, there was no open market if sellers and buyers made bilateral deals, even if these arrangements came about through a bid process. For some market designers, the problem was that there was no defined marketplace where participants might have a wider and ever-changing choice. The strongest market advocates, like Harvard professor William Hogan, the guru of competition, and the energy company Enron, placed greater emphasis on the market than on what customers wanted.

The bilateral deal allowed for a small "net market," allowing customers to buy the small amount they needed in addition to the bilateral supply. While some parts of the country moved to adopt the "net" market, the purists promoting restructuring wanted something more. They preferred a centralized or mandatory "gross" pool in which all power was bought and sold and no bilateral deals were allowed. In theory, the customer would see two results. First, because all power supply would be in play, customers would be expected to see the benefits of having more competitors vying for their business. Second, because all prices would be set in an open market on a relatively short-term basis, customers would get to feel the effects of actual changes in the market resulting from the cost of fuel and the law of supply and demand. The customers would get most of the price risk.

For most customers, the "gross" market is not a good deal. They lose the ability to make their own arrangements; the market does it for them on a uniform basis. They also forfeit the stability in power costs they had derived from longer-term arrangements.

The Tide of Rising Prices

In some states, the early results of the new order were discouraging. Price caps were required to make the new system attractive and to protect customers from a market with no constraints on the price that generation suppliers could charge. Seven states—including

California, whose story became a classic—found that the market structures they had created did not work; they simply suspended what they had started and tried to retreat to the old ways of doing business.

The most catastrophic experience occurred in Montana. Faced with what it believed were great opportunities resulting from restructuring, the misguided Montana Power Company saw a bonanza. It would sell off its generation, transmission, and distribution system, gaining $2.7 billion, an amount apparently well below the true value of the assets sold. Having sold off all of its assets in pieces, Montana Power simply put itself out of business. The proceeds were plowed back into a fiber-optic cable company called Touch America, which soon failed. Those who were truly "touched" were the company shareholders, employees, and customers, all of whom lost almost everything—investment, retirement, good rates. Seldom does an electric utility make the national news, but CBS's *60 Minutes* broadcast a piece called "Who Killed Montana Power?" Actually, it was suicide.

Even in the sixteen or so states, mostly in New England, New York, and the Mid-Atlantic states, where retail competition survived these pitfalls, the major beneficiaries were the large industrial customers. As sophisticated customers, they hardly needed all of the complex rules and market management costs that came along with restructuring. If they had merely been allowed access to the transmission system to purchase power as they chose, as had been the case with natural gas, they would almost certainly have done just as well, without all of the problems that came along with a poorly conceived retail market. Probably the best-functioning retail market was Maine's, because every customer—even those making no decisions—obtained power supply from an independent source selected by competitive bid.

State legislatures also agreed to allow utilities to collect stranded costs, which meant that these costs were added to customers' bills, a pricing policy that stymied the promised benefits of competition. Stranded costs included paying off high-priced PURPA contracts. As a result, the regulators who had erred in setting PURPA's avoided costs too high then forced customers to pay for these mistakes. Adding to the problem, some states allowed the utilities to borrow the money to pay off stranded costs and recover the debt service over a long period. That reduced the immediate impact of stranded cost but also cost the customers even more in the form of interest payments.

Not only did state actions make it likely that retail market access would produce little real benefit in most states, but just as competition was introduced, prices began to rise. The price of fuel— mainly natural gas and oil—was climbing in the world market; hot summers required more air conditioning. The promise of competition was undermined by rising prices.

But state regulators were also at fault. In Texas and several other states, they raised retail rates above their actual cost. Because they had relatively high costs, new generators could sell power only if their offers could beat artificially high prices set for existing generators, so prices were set to make that possible. Texas went too far. In late 2005, an investment group announced that it would sell Texas Genco, a company for which it had paid $900 million a year earlier, for $5.8 billion. Texas Genco produces power generated using coal. The state-mandated market price is pegged to natural gas, which saw a huge price increase in the year and cost far more than coal per kilowatt-hour. The investors collected the difference between the cost of coal and nuclear power and the price of natural gas, while NRG Energy, the purchaser, bet that natural gas would keep producing a healthy margin. The customers received none of the benefit of the price differential but funded the excess profits of the sellers. A local community organizer complained, "the entire situation is terrible, but this one chapter is obscene." The *New York Times* headlined the story: "The Deal That Even Awed Them in Houston" and compared the boldness of it to Enron's "flash and fame."[27]

In Ohio, which claimed to be second only to Texas in exposing its customers to competition, state regulators reported that the process of opening the state to competition was going more slowly than expected. It worked best in those parts of the state where the regulators had set prices high enough for competitors to beat the established utilities. Promoters of competition claimed that existing utilities had inherent advantages that could be overcome only by forcing their prices up. "Where utility prices are already low, suppliers have little room to compete,"[28] said the chairman of the Ohio regulatory body.

When prices are artificially inflated to open the door to competitors, the incumbent utility gets immediate benefit, but the customer gets only a promise that the higher price will attract competitors. The regulators came to believe that competition was an end in itself, completely losing sight of the need to produce better prices. As with PURPA, customers were asked to pay more now in return for better prices later.

The market itself incurred new costs, and these were passed on in transmission rates. The sharply increasing administrative costs of the ISOs trickled down through transmission rates into retail rates. In states where retail access had been adopted and lower prices had been promised, such costs were a burden that helped undermine success. As we shall see below, the states themselves added costs that were tacked onto customers' bills.

Customers Don't Care

Customers traditionally had little say over what they bought or paid for electricity. Those that paid attention depended on state regulators to look out for them. Nothing much changed in a world where they were supposed to be able to exercise choice, although regulators played a reduced role in setting prices.

Not surprisingly, most customers showed a great deal of indifference to the transformation of the power market. A majority showed little interest in shopping for electricity. By taking no action when offered the opportunity, they often found themselves buying "default" power that came from their traditional utility suppliers or that had been purchased on their behalf by an entity, sometimes the state itself. Whatever was happening in the market, customers expected the lights to come on, reliably and at any time, whenever they flipped the switch. So default power, or the "standard offer," as it was called in some places, was essential.

Customers liked default power. If they chose not to select a competitive supplier, they could simply take no action and receive electricity from the default supplier. Often, that supplier was their familiar local utility. By becoming default power purchasers, customers in states where there was retail market access experienced a world in which not much had changed. Perhaps after all the confusion in the telephone business that had followed the breakup of AT&T, they hoped to avoid change by their inaction. Ignoring the fact that people like default service, those promoting competition considered it a badge of honor for a state to have as many of its electricity customers as possible using competitive rather than default power supply.

Residential customers were unknowingly part of the largest customer group in the market. If a utility were prevented by law or regulation from supplying customers from its own generating resources, it would have to offer to buy default power supply on the open market. Suppliers found selling to the default customer group especially attractive because they could count on a highly predictable demand with little risk of losing customers. To the surprise of most industry people, the large class of default customers became the market of choice.

Industrial customers had been thought to be the prime market. But the problem for power marketers is that if they gamble on sales to a single, large customer, they face the risk that a factory might suddenly close or its owner file for bankruptcy protection. The industrial market turned out to be much more difficult than forecast, and the industrial customer found itself having to prove its creditworthiness in ways that it had never faced in the traditional setting. Even worse, factories had to make financial guarantees that they had never before faced. Still, the industrial market produced some of the promised positive results of industry restructuring.

If the consumers were being buffeted by the effects of the struggles to create power markets, the theorists had even more complexity in store for them. Ideally, people should be encouraged to use electricity when overall demand for power is low and reduce their usage when the load on the system is at its peak. While people may not respond to requests to reduce their usage voluntarily, in theory they will use less when its costs more. This is called "real-time pricing." Clearly, this is not a program that is likely to work for the average residential consumer. Few people will start running the clothes washer and dryer at 2:00 AM nor will they forego their favorite prime-time television programs. When a so-called advanced meter appears on the side of the house, ready to measure usage by the hour, it signals the arrival of real-time pricing. Customers must pay for the meter. The way electric rates work, the costs of meters may be collected forever, reducing whatever the savings they were supposed to make possible.

Real-time pricing is best for industrial customers, provided they are given notice of daily changes in prices, to take advantage of the cost savings that result from real-time pricing. For example, a manufacturer might cut its production in peak-cost hours and shift some work to the middle of the night. However, for most customer groups, it adds complexity, further undermining the chances for a successful competitive market environment. There is no apparent reason that buyers and sellers could not work out time-sensitive deals without regulators mandating them. While "time of use" or "real-time" may seem like nothing more than a wrinkle on an already convoluted system, it is likely to become a costly way to achieve doubtful results for many customers.

The supply side of the competitive market remains mostly under the control of the major utilities, whose number has decreased, limiting choice. But with the development of markets, all wholesale customers and some retail customers can purchase power in the competitive market. That raises at least the possibility that customers could set the tone of the market if they could get organized. Groups of customers might, more effectively than individual customers, be able to demand that suppliers bid to provide them power.

Aggregators and the Green Power Scam

Almost from the outset of retail competition, regulators expected small customers to be organized into large purchasing groups by entities called aggregators. Suppliers are expected to be willing to work with aggregators, which should do the hard work of assembling unsophisticated customers into sophisticated groups. Larger groups of customers are attractive to suppliers who might realize economies of scale and might experience more efficient use of their resources if aggregators built purchasing groups.

Perhaps the most significant reason for the lackluster showing of most aggregators is the lack of interest among customers. Competition might have been intended to bring benefits, mainly in the form of lower prices, but most customers seem to prefer to take whatever power supply comes their way and not bother much about the opportunities offered by the market.

Only one group strongly favors aggregators offering competitive power supply, and this relatively small group is willing to pay more than the market price. These people want to purchase "green power"—power supply from renewable resources.

People signing up with aggregators to purchase green power are unlikely to get it, and it is quite possible that they will never know the source of their electricity. The marketing of green power flies in the face of the basic physics of electricity. All generators put electrons into motion, and they can be pushed out onto the grid. All electrons are the same no matter how they are produced. They travel on the transmission grid and on distribution lines until they reach customers who use them to light their rooms and power the motors in their appliances. Electrons do not travel any further than they have to, so that a generator serves customers closest to it, with any excess power moving down the line to the next available customers. This general rule is no less true for the electrons produced by generators fueled by the wind or the sun or falling water than for any other generators. It is mostly a matter of chance whether a customer is supplied from green power resources or any other. It is simply impossible, short of having the generator in your own backyard, to guarantee yourself green power.

Too few customers ask for green power to cause any new environmentally desirable generators to be built. Sometimes hucksters manage to get customers to pay more on the promise of supporting green power, then simply pocket the added profit. It took California a couple of years to put Keystone Energy, just such a scam artist, out of business.

Some states require that competitive power suppliers include in their generation mix a specified amount of power from renewable resources, forcing green power on the customers. These state requirements have done more to keep high-price units as part of the supply than to cause new ones to be added.

Wires Companies and Reddy's Comeback

Some companies like National Grid, a British company that bought U.S. wires companies, and Energy East, a New York–based company, saw their future and their fortune in wires. The existing distribution systems need relatively little new investment, just enough to keep them in operating condition. The key realization for these companies was that existing lines could carry more power without more investment. If these wires had been adequately financed at regulated rates, then each new kilowatt-hour would amount to pure profit as it would entail no additional operating cost.

Reddy Kilowatt would return from his exile when the pure wires companies appeared. Bill inserts, those messages that utilities include in their monthly statement envelopes, gradually began suggesting that air conditioning was good for the customer and that people needed humidifiers (or dehumidifiers). If the wires company could get people to use more electricity, the companies stood to be soundly profitable. In many cases, they could convince state regulators to give them fixed rates on the understanding that they could keep any added profit derived from increased efficiency. Thanks to these "performance-based rates," investors soon got to like these supposedly dull companies, which could produce reliable profits.

Under this system, utilities might gamble that they could cut costs without increasing complaints about declining reliability. Often the prime budget item to suffer is nicely called "vegetation management"—in plain language, tree trimming. Most electric lines are not insulated, and if a branch touches a wire, current is carried to the ground and service is interrupted. If incidents occur infrequently, the utility can get away with little or no tree trimming for many years and keep the money. The prime example of just how badly a utility can perform was the massive blackout of 2003, started when a tree touched a transmission line in Ohio.

The curious result of the coming of retail access was not necessarily lower rates for customers. The biggest winner was likely to be the very utility that was supposed to be the biggest loser. Wires companies, secure in their monopolies and enjoying performance-based regulation, made more money with less pain than ever.

The efforts of the states that authorized retail access to create markets, were well-intentioned but inept. By late 2005, a writer for the *Chicago Tribune* would wonder how Illinois had gone from expectations for lower bills to a 35 percent increase. The legislatively mandated reduction of 20 percent in prices had created the expectations, but the costs did not follow the prices down. The prime sponsor of the state's restructuring legislation was forced to admit, "There really wasn't a great demand for a competitive residential market."[29]

In the luckiest of the retail-access states, possibly the best possible result that could be achieved was that nothing much changed. Among the states taking the most aggressive steps to create retail markets, the worst result would come from the biggest state.

The Restructuring Alphabet

EWG: Exempt Wholesale Generator, a generator that may be owned by a utility even if such ownership would be banned by PUHCA. Authorized in the 1992 EPAct but made unnecessary by the repeal of PUHCA in 2005.

ISO: Independent System Operator, a nonprofit FERC-authorized entity that may operate and control transmission lines owned by others and that is not owned by any market participant. A nongovernmental agency regulated by FERC but exercising government-like authority.

ITC: Independent transmission company, an entity that may own and operate transmission lines and that is not owned by any other type of market participant.

LICAP/RPM: Locational Installed Capacity or Regional Pricing Model. A system under which customers are required to pay added costs to attract generators to a market area with limited transmission access to other areas.

MISO: Mid-West Independent System Operator

NEPOOL: New England Power Pool, a utility group that ran a power exchange before EPAct but has been supplanted by ISO-New England.

OASIS: Open Access Same-time Information System; transmission operators, including ISOs and RTOs are required to post on the Internet information about the short-term and long-term use of their transmission systems.

PJM: An ISO in the Mid-Atlantic region.

RTO: Regional Transmission Operator, similar to ISO, but with enhanced powers of control over transmission systems owned by others. May also own systems.

SMD: Standard Market Design, an unsuccessful FERC initiative to impose a single set of rules to govern all electricity trading in the United States. In its absence, regions have different sets of rules.

CHAPTER 5

CALIFORNIA MEETS ENRON

K en Lay was a great success in the natural gas business. In 1986, he was chosen to be the chairman of a natural gas company that he would quickly rename Enron. Among the people Lay hired was Jeff Skilling, who had been a management consultant but quickly rose to running the company on a day-to-day basis. Based on the company's success in trading natural gas and the prospects for the restructured electricity industry, Skilling wanted Enron to get into the electric business a far larger industry than natural gas.[30]

At the moment of its conception, Enron's entry into the electric business had a fatal flaw. Skilling wanted the company to sell and trade the output of generators owned by others, but he did not want Enron to own any physical assets itself. Perhaps his decision was motivated by the company's proven understanding of natural gas trading and by its complete unfamiliarity with the electric business.

Perhaps it was motivated by the belief that investing in generation took too much capital and involved too much risk. But when, in the mid-1990s, Enron approached utilities that owned generation, those companies rejected Enron's proposal in part because Skilling was ahead of his time. They were used to selling their own power and preferred to continue doing so.

But Enron did not drop the matter. By 1996, FERC was in the final phases of issuing an order to govern open transmission access, paving the way for any entity to use the grid to move power. Electricity trading was about to become a much bigger business, because companies would no longer need to be utilities in order to use the grid.

Skilling had brought Andy Fastow, a banker with expertise in financing complex deals, onto the Enron corporate staff and had asked him to come up with a strategy for entry into the retail electric business, which many in the industry believed would inevitably follow the start of wholesale access. In fact, marketing outfits, led by Enron, would lobby hard in states across the country to get legislatures to authorize retail competition. At first Fastow struggled unsuccessfully to come up with an idea that would make Enron a major player in the emerging retail business.

Fastow's Follies

Fastow came up with a strategy based on making guesses about the course of industry restructuring. He believed that regulatory changes would lead to real competition and that competition would lead to lower prices. He believed that this would take place; he did not know it. His idea was to enter into long-term contracts with major retail customers at prices below what they were paying— an offer surely attractive to them—and fulfill the contracts by purchasing power on the open market, where prices would have fallen by the time Enron had to deliver.

What Fastow ignored was that the emerging market would be transparent. People would be able to figure out what Enron was doing. First, it would be obvious that the company would be losing money unless and until the prices it paid fell as Fastow had forecasted. Second, customers could soon understand that they had signed themselves up for deals that actually ripped them off.

To compound these problems, Fastow wanted to cushion the company from the inevitable start-up losses by hedging the risk. But hedges cannot protect against a poor business design, and none could be developed. Even if electricity were regarded as a commodity, hedges might at best protect only against its prices going in the wrong direction. Nothing could protect Enron against a flawed business design that would not work, as there was no way it could survive market scrutiny.

Yet Enron went ahead with Fastow's concept—in a big way. It invested in a large staff, including lobbyists in many states who pushed for the most extreme open-market conditions with all customer protection relying on the supposed efficiency of the market. There would be no requirement that a supplier have generators at its disposal and no charge for demand, only for energy. Companies would be allowed to bid to provide services such as meter reading and billing. Enron wanted revolution, not merely change. It opened a huge trading operation at its Houston headquarters. It marketed power aggressively to large national customers.

Enron's competitors were shaken by its apparent success. It was offering prices to potential customers that were not justified by the actual cost of supply from the generators. It was plain that Enron was operating at a loss to gain market share. Unless you had access to the kind of financing available to Enron, you could not compete with the company. Perhaps what Enron was doing constituted predatory pricing, but matters were moving too quickly for any competitor to have a realistic hope that it could get the federal government to stop Enron. A competitor could only assume either that Enron would simply have to fall into line with market reality, making it less of a problem as a competitor, or that it had discovered some revolutionary business concept that would make its gamble pay off.

But one of Fastow's seemingly weak ideas appeared to work just as he had planned. Many large companies to which Enron pitched its long-term deals seemed quite willing to accept a lower price than they had been paying without thinking about how Enron could pull it off. A company might also like the idea of one-stop shopping, with Enron as the sole supplier in place of many local utilities. Big names readily signed up. And they signed contracts that were put before them after they had already accepted a price. They were given as little as a day to agree to the terms of the deal. It was perhaps a perfect match between Enron's greed and that of its customers.

More careful customers resisted Enron's siren song. Enron's salespeople were so inexperienced that a prudent purchaser would be worried. The essence of the electric industry was always that a supplier must have enough generating capacity, measured in kilowatts, available to produce the power needed at the moment of highest demand. The electrons a generator puts onto the grid are energy measured in kilowatt-hours. At Enron, sales people did not know the difference between a kilowatt and a kilowatt-hour. But a customer, enthralled by the Enron offer and whose knowledge of electricity was limited to knowing the amount of its monthly bill, might not care and would accept the deal.

Enron's entry into the electric market was, well, electrifying. Here was a company that owned no generating assets and no wires but could not be ignored. Its confidence, its apparent innovation, and its aggressive business style made it a major force in a newly emerging business. No competitor could throw its money around as Enron did nor enter as many emerging markets. Enron was quickly becoming the standard by which competition in the electric industry was measured. Few suspected that under the surface there was no innovative new business concept and that the company was losing money every day. It was a classic case of buying a reputation using other people's money.

What Enron was doing was playing the market, a way of providing electric power that had never been tried previously. Traditionally, utilities owned generators or had the right to sufficient generator output to meet their obligations to their customers. In the wholesale business, a power company had the resources to meet the full requirements of the retail utility buying from it. The introduction of the competitive market usually meant a small but significant change. As we have seen, the supplier would continue to meet its obligations by holding a portfolio of generation and then supplementing it for marginal or occasional needs by making purchases in a short-term market. Eventually, entities that were not traditional utilities—marketers—would come to play the same role. But most power supply remained as it had always been—asset-based. Except for Enron.

Enron owned no generation nor did it hold long-term rights to generation owned by others. It owned virtually no industry assets except for Portland General Electric, an Oregon utility it had acquired almost as an aberration at a time when it sought, usually unsuccessfully, tangible holdings. Its basic electric business was a pure trading operation and was unique for its complete reliance on the market. The company thought that it knew energy markets so well that it could beat competitors that were burdened by the financial obligations of actually owning and operating facilities. That worked for natural gas, where presumably Enron was a competent trader; it did not work for electricity, and Enron took too long figuring that out.

Customers were somewhat bewildered by the way Enron did business. It would quote a price for a contract, even a ten-year deal, that held good for only one day. A purchaser might legitimately wonder how the price for a lengthy purchase could be radically affected from one day to another, especially when there had been no news suggesting any major change in the cost of fuel to generate electricity. The largest single customer in New England simply walked away from Enron after an abrupt and seemingly unwarranted increase in the quoted price, believing that it had been the victim of a bait-and-switch operation.

Customers dealing with Enron would soon find that the deal was being determined by people they never met, the people on the trading desk. The sales staff carried messages between the potential customers and the traders who actually set the price. At the heart of the game was the effort by traders to hedge the cost of the power supply they would purchase in the future to meet their commitment. This was a high-risk game, because Enron could enter into a multiyear commitment without having any idea where it would purchase the power to fulfill its obligation.

The traders' principal task, it seemed, was to hedge Enron's purchase price so that it could be assured of a profit margin on every kilowatt-hour it sold. The problem was that the company could not hedge a long-term sale. It might hedge the price, protecting itself from an unexpected change in the spot market, for several months, but not much longer. So it engaged in the practice of "stacked" hedges, entering into a new hedge arrangement at the expiration of the old over the life of the contract. That was why the price of a long-term contract could be so greatly affected by a change in the short-term market. Enron simply had no way of knowing anything more than the short-term price.

The method was only as good as the hedges themselves. Outsiders could readily believe that Enron must have found the key to sophisticated hedging by having developed an incredible grasp of how to counter changes in the prices of electricity. But what if the hedges were not financial hedges at all, but simply gambles on what the price of electricity would be, determined mostly by expectations about the cost of the fuels necessary to generate it and the tightness of supply in the future market. Fastow remained confident that the price of electricity would fall because of industry restructuring and the hedges, but he had no knowledge of the business and was consequently ignorant about just how much or how little power would be traded in the emerging market.

This combination of ignorance and arrogance was compounded by the nature of the market itself. For one thing, there was much less of a market than Enron had thought there would be. In financial terms, the market was illiquid. Electricity does not trade like natural gas because it is not really a commodity. Some degree of spot trading is possible, but contracts cannot reasonably be hedged for more than about eighteen months. And there is much less power being traded in most markets than would be necessary to create a truly liquid market. Finally, Enron had not discovered any unique way to hedge the price of electricity and took big risks on imperfect insurance.

Enron portrayed itself as the promoter of full and open competition, and its legions of lobbyists pushed continually for the fewest legal constraints on the business and away from any requirements that marketers own assets or the rights to them in favor of complete reliance on the market. If you believed in competition and open markets, all of this sounded good, and Enron got much credit for taking the lead in promoting the kind of competition that had been intended by EPAct. There was little concern about its policies, though some thought that change might be taking place too fast. Few realized that the results Enron sought were desperately needed if it were to survive in the business. If there were not a liquid market in electricity, with substantial quantities changing hands virtually daily, Enron faced the prospect that Fastow's price predictions would be all wrong, that hedging would not work, and that the company would hemorrhage cash. What Enron needed was a large and essentially short-term market with a sufficient number of other players who had no choice but to sell to that market and thus supply Enron with the power it needed at the price it expected so that it could keep its commitments.

In most areas of the country, no such markets developed, and Enron was left trying to make its incompetent hedging work—not that any potential customer knew there were any problems. Enron threw its weight and its money around with supreme confidence, and the prices it offered seemed attractive. The company had thought it could reap larger profits from selling power than it learned were possible. Many costs of the electric business—notably the poles and wires—are fixed and not subject to movement in the generation market. And the price of generation itself has to take into account the fixed costs of the generator. As a result, the scope of the market in which competitive pricing has an effect is a lot thinner than Enron had thought. Its solution was to try for larger markets and to do so by leaving the impression that all was working well. Enron was scamming customers and legislators. Internally, Enron was acting like that classic, nonsense business case: a company that could not make a profit selling a product would try to make it up in volume.

As Enron could not make its electric business work correctly and legally, it would simply bend or break rules and laws to produce a profit—or at least, what seemed to be one. One practice that ran through virtually all that Enron did was false reporting. It would make it look as though its electric business was profitable by falsely reporting success. It accomplished that sleight of hand by using a method called "mark to market," a legal process not unique to Enron but completely misleading in its case. It would show as current revenue the income from a power sales contract that might extend for years. At the same time, it could only estimate the future cost of fulfilling the contract or, even worse, would simply include only its current costs. The results looked strongly positive to investors. Arthur Anderson LLP, Enron's accountants, went along with this aggressive financial reporting, and many in the investment community found it acceptable because it kept the boom of the late 1990s going at full speed. Financial reporting, intended to help investors protect themselves, was the casualty.

But if these accounting games were legal, although dubious, Enron had no problem with clear violations of the rules governing the market. A New England rule required it to sign up for generating capacity to go along with its energy imports from outside the region. Though it had been informed in writing of this rule, it failed to buy rights to generation. When caught by the ISO, Enron feigned ignorance. The ISO found Enron liable for compensating for its action by making additional payments of about $10 million, though the company finally convinced the ISO to settle for far less. As usual, its accounting games kept the matter from being disclosed to its investors, but the arrogant and blatant violation reduced the value of the investment. Management apparently simply chalked the matter up to experience, if it did even that.

California, Here We Come

Then Enron came to California. In 1996, the state had set up its market. GOP governor Pete Wilson believed, as did Andy Fastow, that competition among generators would cause prices to fall. So sure was California of this assumption that the state legislature mandated a 10 percent cut in rates locked in for five years. Apparently, the politicians had been impressed by the supposed success of the restructured British market and decided to skip over the growing pains, apply as much of that experience as possible, and mandate the benefits immediately. The policy was good politics but bad economics.

At first, Enron did not like the rules, because too much was set in stone. Gradually it came to realize that the rules worked in its favor because, despite the state's cap on retail rates, there was no cap on the price of the power sold to utilities. The utilities saw that they would be squeezed by this system, but their complaints were ignored as coming from, in Wilson's words, an "outdated monopoly."[31]

In the summer of 2000, California began to experience temperatures over 100 degrees Fahrenheit. Demand for electricity, mostly for air conditioning, soared with the thermometer. The California ISO either had to come up with power supply to meet the demand or had to get customers to shut off some equipment voluntarily. It scrambled to do both.

The daily market worked according to a bid system. Power supply prices were no longer based on the cost of production plus a limited profit margin but reflected what the market would bear. Traditionally, as the demand had increased, less efficient and more costly generators were brought on line. Now, similarly, as the ISO looked for more power, it would have to pay higher prices, not because the cost of generation required it but because the law of supply and demand did. The ISO was authorized to deal only with power supply being offered in the California market, but could not require an in-state generator to serve the state's customers if it already had made commitments to others elsewhere.

As demand increased, the ISO found that some generators were out of service and others had already been committed to serve customers outside California. The power from some generators could not get to customers needing it, because the lines were full, or "congested." Prices inevitably rose as the ISO was forced to pay whatever the market demanded, ultimately up to a cap of 75 cents per kilowatt-hour, more than ten times what end-use customers usually paid. The ISO spread its purchasing out to neighboring states with the effect of exporting its own crisis and driving prices up as far away as Washington state. Nobody was happy. The utilities were squeezed and knew they would have a battle to be compensated for the losses that were caused by a policy requiring them to pay market prices for power but charge lower, regulated prices to end-use customers. Those utilities that could let their prices float up to a cap saw them rise. The cap increased and affected customers found they had to cut back consumption and pay high prices just when they needed air conditioning the most. The California Public Utilities Commission reported that customers had paid more than $1 billion more during June and July than they had a year earlier. The ISO was frustrated. Political leaders were facing responsibility for a flawed system that had not realized its promise. The PUC reported that it was possible that the market was being manipulated by unscrupulous traders.

In the midst of this chaos, somebody was happy. Enron exploited this situation beyond any limits ever anticipated and, more important, beyond the ability of the ISO to do anything about it. First, it would make a reservation on the transmission grid for sales of power that would never take place. "If the line's not congested I just look to congest it. . . . If you can congest it, that's a moneymaker no matter what,"[32] said one Enron employee over the recorded trading line. The traders knew they were "gaming the system," taking advantage of the rules and their administration to come up with profitable results that were not part of the original market design. "So, uh, somebody's figured out how to set congestion?" a trader asked the Enron desk in Portland, Oregon. "Well, we . . . we can set it if we want. I mean, it's not a hard game to do." Faced with Enron's reservations for use of the transmission lines, which the ISO did not recognize as phony, the ISO could not schedule use of the lines for desperately needed power supply. The ISO might find out too late that the reserved transmission access was not being used and was now available. FERC had thought in terms of reservations being made days or months in advance; Enron was working hour by hour. It was an uneven game, with the ISO following its own and FERC's rules, and Enron flouting them.

"Do you know when you started overscheduling and making buckets of money on that?" asked one Enron trader.

If it wanted to drive up the price, Enron would induce California generators whose power was committed simply to shut down. Generating units sometimes have to go out of service because of an operational failure, but such shutdowns are particularly painful when supplies are tight. Enron used artificial problems to cause shutdowns, making supplies tight.

"I was wondering, um, the demand out there is, er . . . there's not much, ah demand for power at all and we're running kind of fat. Um, if you took down the steamer [generator], how long would it take to get it back up?" an Enron trader asked.

"Of, it's not something you want to just be turning on and off every hour. Let's put it that way," a generator operator replied.

"If we shut it down, could you bring it back up in three—three or four hours, something like that?"

"Oh, yeah," answered the other operator.

"Well, why don't you just go ahead and shut her down then, if that's OK," came the order.

To prevent more power coming from the Pacific Northwest, Enron traders pushed what they laughingly called the "tree hugger button." By claiming that salmon were endangered by the operation of certain hydro generators, they caused the facilities to be shut down.

On a day of rolling blackouts in California, an Enron trader managed to get a plant to go off-line in neighboring Nevada:

> **Enron:** Ah, we want you guys to get a little creative.
>
> **El Paso Electric Company Operator:** OK.
>
> **Enron:** And come up with a reason to go down.
>
> **Operator:** OK.
>
> **Enron:** Anything you want to do over there? Any. . . .
>
> **Operator:** Ah . . .
>
> **Enron:** Cleaning, anything like that?
>
> **Operator:** Yeah. Yeah. There's some stuff we could be doing.

Besides phony reservations and induced shutdowns, the third element of Enron's market manipulation was its power laundering. It would ship power from California to Oregon or other out-of-state locations and then bring it back into California. It would disguise the source to make it seem that the power supply was coming from Oregon generators. Because only California generators were subject to the new state price cap on supply, Enron could charge whatever the market would bear for the supposed imports. It was reported to have made profits of more than $222,000 on one such transaction that lasted for only three hours.[33]

Enron's schemes, with names like "sidewinder," "ping pong,"

"donkey punch," and "Russian roulette," extended even to Alberta, Canada, which was part of the same interconnected market. Evidence later showed that Jeff Skilling himself was aware of the Canadian "Project Stanley," possibly named after professional ice hockey's Stanley Cup, the pride of Canada. At least one tape proved that the traders knew what they were doing was illegal.

John Lavorato, in charge of Project Stanley: "I'm just ah—fuck, I'm just trying to be an honest camper so I only go to jail once."

Tim Belden, head of the Enron Portland operation who would actually plead guilty later: "Well, there you go. At least in only one country" [laughter].

Lavorato: "Yeah, fuck, this isn't a joke. I'm a tide—nobody else seems to be concerned anymore about, except me."

Belden: "Yeah."

The Enron traders knew what they were doing was illegal, but they believed that Ken Lay's close friendship with President Bush and Vice President Cheney would assure that they would be immune from any sanction. Their arrogance was manifested by their willingness to have their conversations recorded.

Every once in a while the Enron traders could put their feet up and savor their success, which often came at the price of human suffering. One recorded voice mused about "all the money you guys stole from those poor grandmothers of California." Enron replied: "Yeah, Grandma Millie, man. But she's the one who couldn't figure out how to fucking vote on the butterfly ballot." Translation: If old ladies were too stupid to know how to vote for Al Gore in Florida, they deserved to suffer in California at the hands of the friends of George Bush.

Enron had almost certainly been the first to play these games, having tested its tricks two years before, putting the squeeze on California. It was the most massive player, but it was not alone.

Reliant Energy of Houston pulled most of the power supply under its control off the market just to drive up prices. One of its traders admitted: "Everybody thought it was really exciting that we were gonna play some market power."[34] Others who preyed upon California included Duke Energy, Portland General Electric, owned by Enron, and Mirant Corp, a Southern Company spin-off that, like Enron, would soon slide from gluttony to bankruptcy.

The Governor Fights and Falls

Governor Gray Davis, Wilson's Democratic successor, knew that the state had problems and was sure that they had been caused by market manipulation. When he complained loudly, he got little comfort from Washington. California officials went to FERC, asking for its intervention and refunds of charges to customers and utilities who seemed to have overpaid. But the federal regulators had not uncovered any evidence of wrongdoing and believed that prices had simply risen because of tight supply. FERC also questioned whether it had any authority to order refunds to be made by generators and marketers, entities that were now supposed to be unregulated. When Davis talked with Federal Reserve Chairman Alan Greenspan and Treasury Secretary Lawrence Summers he got no more comfort. They believed that prices had to be allowed to rise so that customers would be under economic pressure to conserve when the temperature rose.[35]

As it happened, the temperature that was rising the most was Davis's. He believed that he was being told to take politically impossible steps by people who had no sense of California's political reality. He could not simply let prices rise wherever they wanted to go. He could not dismantle environmental laws in order to allow new power plants to be thrown up. Given the state's referendum habit, he could easily find himself overruled by unhappy voters. And worst of all, he could not accept the belief that what was happening to his state's electricity customers was just the effect of the open market at work and not the result of illegal market manipulation.

As the crisis continued, FERC wavered. It had wanted to let the market operate without its intervention but found that the crisis would continue while power could be shifted from one state to another to earn the marketers the best profits. That might be a market operation of sorts, but it made California into everybody's sugar daddy. Reluctantly, more than a year after the crisis had begun, FERC instituted a price cap all across the West. The crisis cooled.

Without relenting in its complaints, California took remedial action. Environmental regulation was accelerated to allow for decisions on building new power plants to be made at top speed. And Davis took some advice he had been given by Skilling in one of their crisis meetings. He decided that the daily market was the culprit and moved aggressively to have California utilities enter into long-term power supply arrangements. So eager was the state to get its power supply firmed up that it recklessly entered into the new contracts at prices that were far too high. California concluded fifty-nine contracts for ten years of power supply at prices more than double what the market would settle at. There might not be blackouts any longer, but customers were bound to suffer. Ken Lay, a good Republican, had urged Davis to blame the crisis on Wilson, his GOP predecessor. The daily market could be laid at Wilson's feet, but not the high-priced long-term contracts. Davis was merely substituting one crisis for another. To make matters worse, instead of sympathizing with California's demand for refunds, FERC actually blamed the state and the ISO for the crisis. It refused to allow Davis to renegotiate the contracts, although later voluntary accords brought some relief as the state's claims against power suppliers were settled.

Oddly enough, among the victims were the state's electric utilities. Caught in the ongoing squeeze between high supply prices and limits of retail prices, they ran out of money. Southern California Edison and Pacific Gas and Electric, formerly stalwarts of the industry, were driven into bankruptcy. For a while, utilities found themselves the target of a bizarre regulatory requirement. Having purchased power at unauthorized high prices, the utilities themselves had violated FERC rules, though they had no choice in the matter. They were told to refund $270 million to the same companies that had gouged their customers. This requirement was never dropped but was largely resolved in the settlements between the state and the renegade marketers.

Finally, retail restructuring in California, a state that had been too arrogant in setting up its market to listen to any more conservative advice, was brought to an end. With long-term supply contracts and new generators coming on line, the utilities began acting much as they had in the past, though they could do little to dictate the price of power. What had started as a much-heralded model power market had ended in ignominy.

The downfall of Enron was caused only in part by its role in manipulating the California market. Driven by the same hubris that had led it to believe it could get away with cheating Grandmother Millie, the company had committed a great many illegal acts across its broad range of operations. Lay and Skilling fell, and the bankrupt company could do little to repair its image. Enron's adverse impact had been felt as far away as the East Coast. When it failed, it could no longer acquire power supply to meet its contractual commitments. Customers who had planned on power supply at Enron's promised prices were suddenly thrown onto the open market, where they often faced added and unexpected costs. Enron became a dirty word.

Enron's collapse brought to an end two major elements of the power market. First, Enron had been almost unique as a supplier with almost no physical assets. In the beginning it had been a marvel of the industry. At the end, no customer would purchase power from an entity unless it owned generation or the firm rights to generation. There would be no more Enrons. Second, in the traditional electric market, transactions had not been secured by financial performance guarantees. A company's history and actual performance had been generally good enough. From now on, both buyers and sellers of power would expect to face contractual requirements proving they could make good on their commitments. Such changes would make for a stronger market, though they had been achieved at high cost.

Enron's investors recovered some of their losses, because financial institutions that had supported the company's illegal operations came up with billions of dollars instead of facing damaging lawsuits. But customers were less likely to be compensated. California had long complained about FERC's failure to deal with the crisis and market manipulation. By 2003, the federal regulators agreed that Enron and others had "gamed" the market. It ordered refunds, although in amounts well below what California had consistently claimed. California finally took FERC to court, winning a ruling from a U.S. Circuit Court that the commission had abdicated its regulatory authority.[36] But the courts left it to Enron to work its way out of the problem rather than ordering remedial action themselves.

Enron settled with state officials in California, Oregon, and Washington for $1.52 billion, far less than California's long-standing claims for more than $8 billion. Other companies came up with compensation or dropped demands for unpaid bills, and some were actually able to come up with the cash to pay for the settlements. There was little likelihood that Enron's customers would ever receive much of what had been promised in the settlement once the bankruptcy case concluded.

Jeff Skilling and Ken Lay were indicted in 2004 for abuses, including providing investors with false and overly optimistic information about the company. Lay claimed he did not know about the California business and a lot of other company wrongdoing, raising the question of whether he would be held responsible for Enron's acts when he was in charge, whether or not he knew the details. The Enron case dragged on in sharp contrast to the federal government's pursuit of Bernard Ebbers, the fallen chief of the communications company WorldCom. Either the prosecutors were having a difficult time putting a case together against Enron's top brass, or there were residual benefits in being the president's friend.

Gray Davis was recalled as governor by California voters mainly because of the huge burden of state debt. Some of that debt was caused by the above-market-priced power supply it had purchased in its haste to line up long-term contracts. Davis had been unable to take Lay's advice and place all the blame on Pete Wilson, because a poorly conceived Republican policy had been replaced under the Democratic governor by one that was not much better. Davis paid the political price, but the customers got to pay the bills.

Ironically, by the summer of 2005, California was again looking at an energy crisis. Some plants tripped out of service, and imports from neighboring states threatened to overload transmission lines. GOP governor Arnold Schwarzenegger, who succeeded Davis after the voters recalled him, could do no better. California had not yet solved its problems.

The California case provides the best evidence of the failure of electric industry restructuring. Refusing to heed the example of other open-access transmission arrangements, the state chose to move to a system where full faith was given to market mechanisms to insure honest competition. California state government officials and regulators failed to consider the ways that the new system might cause results different from traditional industry practice and certainly never foresaw the possibility of massive gaming of the system. Even worse, by denying people the right to enter into long-term contracts, the system regulated customer choice, the very objective of restructuring the industry. Finally, when the system collapsed, the governor panicked and fled to long-term, high-cost contracts, and FERC tried to ignore what was happening in the belief that nothing was really wrong with the market. While the federal regulators might be accused of aiding the president's friends, it seemed more likely that they had simply come to believe too much in their own rhetoric about the virtues of competition.

CHAPTER 6

THE BLACKOUT

Martha Burns did not like the prospect of sleeping on the marble floor of Manhattan's MetLife Building. Nor was she looking forward to sharing the night with thousands of people who had crowded into the building because Grand Central Station was closed to the public. She wanted to be back home in Westchester with her husband, not forced to spend a wakeful night in the eerie glow of emergency lights.

Martha had put in another of her long days as the business manager of her husband's one-man law practice. He had left their Manhattan office early and caught the train home. But on the afternoon of August 14, 2003, Martha was still in the office clearing up paperwork when, at about 4:30 P.M. the lights went out. This was no minor inconvenience; it was the start of a major blackout. Martha had to climb down eleven flights of stairs and walk to Grand Central Station, only to find that commuters were being diverted to the adjoining MetLife office building. She had no idea how long she would have to camp for the night on the cold, hard floor.

Eventually, the blackout turned out not to be more than a major inconvenience for Martha. Her husband was on a train pulled by a diesel engine, which, though caught between two dead electric-powered trains, was able to back up to a station. There he caught a ride with a woman who had been able to call her husband to pick her up. Back in Manhattan, MetLife made a phone bank available to the stranded passengers; Martha contacted her husband, who drove into New York City to pick her up, along with a group of people also stranded in Manhattan. Martha made it home.

Millions suffered the same distress as Martha, but for others it was much worse. The economic cost of the blackout could never be calculated but was estimated as being between $4 billion and $10 billion in the United States, with additional costs in Canada, which actually suffered a one-month recession because of the loss of power. What would turn out to have been a simple problem with the transmission grid had caused widespread harm and had sent a message that worse was possible.

The lights in Martha's office went out when the power grid in New York shut down, leaving the city in a state of suspended animation. She and millions of others were victims of a chain of events that had started hundreds of miles away. After life ground to a halt, it recovered just enough for people to find out what had happened.

Beginning about twenty minutes before the lights went out in Martha's office, portions of the giant power lines that feed the northeastern United States had begun to shut down. Nobody knew why. Even worse, nobody knew what to do about it. Fortunately, the outage happened on an afternoon when the sun provided plenty of natural light and warmth, so people were spared a catastrophe.

The blackout hit a large part of the Northeast—Ohio, Michigan, Pennsylvania, New York, New Jersey, and small parts of other neighboring states; Ontario, Canada's most populous province, went black with virtually no power. Authorities rushed out with estimates that about 50 million people, more than the entire population of Spain, had been left without electricity. People at work set about trying to get home. Many had used mass transportation to get to work and now had to trudge home on foot. Those with cars took to the road. Only four years before, in an event that was also troublesome but localized to northern Manhattan, New Yorkers had lived through another blackout, so they were learning. They coped.

The blackout of 2003 was not much more than a major inconvenience for most people like Martha Burns. The great majority could live without power for a while. But there were reports of deaths, fires, and substantial economic loss. The shutdown of air conditioning, in a country that had become heavily dependent on it caused considerable harm. Many people were deeply concerned, mindful that such an event in the depth of winter would have caused great hardship and worried about whether there was a greater threat, such as terrorism, behind the outage.

What had happened? The Canadian prime minister, Jean Chrétien, said he thought the problems in Ontario had been imported from the United States. The first words out of Washington were that it was the fault of Ontario. With relations between the two countries already battered, the instant retaliatory response by the United States was neither surprising nor based in fact. True, the blackout had hit Ontario before it reached New York, but Washington chose to ignore the irrefutable finding by the Ontario electric utility that it had been affected by problems from south of the border.

Washington's initial statement was not the only wild claim made in the first few hours. Television news began reporting an even

wider loss of power than had actually happened, and the broad-
casts' hastily generated maps were based more on rumor than sound
reporting. The inaccurate reporting may have amused those who
were watching the news shows when they were supposed to be
unable to do so, but it also increased the sense of alarm. Former
Energy Secretary Bill Richardson, from a safe distance in Santa Fe as
governor of New Mexico, issued his verdict: "We are a major super-
power with a third-world electric grid. Our grid is antiquated. It
needs serious modernization."[37]

Another instant response was that the grid had simply become
overloaded on a hot summer day. Some thought that a summer
heat wave, with air conditioners running full blast, called for
more electricity than the lines could carry or than could get
through the transmission bottlenecks that had arisen in the past
few years.

The facts would soon prove most of the alarmist news and free-
ranging comment wrong. The transmission system is not "antiquated." The liability exposure for utilities would be too great for
them to allow the lines to deteriorate to the point that they could be
a danger to life and property. In fact, their annual reports to regulators showed that as a whole, transmission lines were less than
halfway through their thirty-year depreciable lives. The poles and
wires were regularly maintained and had achieved a high degree of
reliability. The summer's day had been no hotter than many others.

The claims that the system is antiquated and that, more plau-
sibly, there is a bottleneck problem were offered as immediate
answers to provide some comfort by implying that all that had to
be done was to replace the antiquated grid with more and better
high-tension lines. Both comments were meant to send the message
that the problem was the people themselves, who wanted more
power but opposed building more power lines. Maybe that old

comic-page character Pogo was right when he had said: "We have met the enemy, and he is us." It was all the fault of environmentalists. That way, no blame attached to the industry itself, much less to government.

Though the power lines are not too old, there may not be enough of them. The electric industry has long known that some bottlenecks exist on the network of high-voltage lines carrying power from dams, nuclear plants, and units fueled by natural gas, coal, or oil to the customers. But it had been believed that blackouts would not be a problem. That was because this situation had occurred before, and the industry itself claimed to have fixed the problem.

The First Big Blackout and the Coming of NERC

On November 9, 1965, at 5:16 P.M., a single line tripped at the Sir Adam Beck Station No. 2 in Ontario, and by 5:27 ;, the outage had cascaded into New York City. Some 30 million people were left without electricity for as long as thirteen hours. The first major American blackout was big news, giving rise to the titillating, but entirely false, story that the birth rate jumped exactly nine months later. It was the basis for a 1968 movie called *Where Were You When the Lights Went Out?* And it led to industry measures designed to prevent such a blackout from ever happening again.

Nobody believes that it will ever be possible to prevent electric utility outages altogether. Some outages are caused by natural events, and it would cost customers too much to pay for utility measures that would dampen the effect of these events and allow prompt recovery. For example, after the widespread blackout of 1998, when millions in the Northeast and Canada went without power for as long as two weeks because of an ice storm, some consumers demanded that transmission lines be put underground.

These demands went nowhere because of the enormous cost, about ten times as much as the cost of overhead lines.

But the blackout of 1965 was not caused by an act of nature, and something could be done to prevent a recurrence. In 1966, the Federal Power Commission proposed that it should be given the authority to regulate the operation of major transmission lines, which until then had been left entirely under utility control. A year later, just after a Northeast blackout affecting 13 million people, the FPC sent detailed proposals to Congress, including asking for the ability to set standards for the reliability, planning, and operations of transmission lines. It would also be able to require the construction of new lines. The Johnson administration proposed to relieve the utilities of some risk by promising limited antitrust exemption to those joining regional transmission planning councils. The FPC said that such councils were essential to insuring reliability and that it would have a representative on each one. Almost all of these proposals would be adopted, but not until thirty-five years later.

The major utilities responded to the FPC in fury. Saying that they alone were competent to regulate transmission reliability, they immediately set about creating a self-regulatory body designed to forestall any federal action. The president of American Electric Power System, in 1967 the largest electric utility, went as far as to suggest that most electric utilities should be eliminated because they were "obsolete, wasteful and an expensive anachronism."[38] The industry giants created the National Electric Reliability Council (NERC) (later to become the North American Electric Reliability Council to reflect the inclusion of Canadian and Mexican members). Despite another New England blackout in 1969, the utilities again succeeded in convincing Congress that they were the ones best able to insure reliability. With the arrival of the Nixon administration, the proposal for a federal role in maintaining reliability was killed.

This victory for the large power companies was symptomatic of the state of regulation itself. Regulators were not technically competent, focusing mainly on rate-setting and later on transmission and market rules. The utilities could argue that they had the expertise and that they could self-regulate. Under this system, there was no sanction for failure to provide reliable electric service. And nobody represented the consumers.

NERC became an industry club, composed of well-meaning technical experts who reported to utilities anxious to keep government at bay. Technical experts from those utilities that chose to join NERC—and eventually almost all did—labored to develop operating standards designed to improve operations and monitoring and to stop cascades when outages occurred. Technically, much of the work done by NERC committees was sound and intended to accomplish its stated purposes. But the new standards were constantly being tweaked, were not mandatory, and nobody policed them. They were often stated in vague generalities that allowed for a wide range of interpretation. The intentions were good, but the utilities had room to avoid compliance.

Even more alarming, while technical developments made it increasingly possible to improve the grid's integrity, companies reluctant to spend the money on upgrades made sure that no censure attached to failure to adopt the new measures. What the industry calls "fast-acting automatic load shedding," or dropping customers quickly to reduce load, was not used in many places. More sophisticated systems that could better protect the grid were available but rarely used. No regulator required them, although everybody knew about them. Implicitly the regulators accepted the verdict of the industry and decided that customers would rather live through blackouts than pay to reduce the chance of them.

The creation of NERC provided false comfort. For the first time, the industry was focusing on grid reliability across interconnected systems and adopting standards to prevent future transmission crashes. NERC was promoted as the model of self-regulation, designed to show that once a problem had been identified, government could leave it to the power companies to deal with it. Utility engineers congregated at its committee meetings and plunged into a depth of detail. The trouble was that NERC leadership made sure that no recommendations came forth that would put great pressure on utility management to introduce expensive reform measures. And utility executives told regulators, at the infrequent moments when they were asked about reliability, that NERC was taking care of business. Nobody regulated NERC.

In a few places in the United States, especially in the Northeast, utilities went further than NERC and took effective action. For example, utility companies in the six New England states created the New England Power Pool (NEPOOL) and agreed to abide by decisions made by the regional organization. This institution, one of only three of its kind, was called a "tight pool," because its governing body could vote to adopt rules by which all agreed to abide. One of its rules required that before a new generator could be linked to the NEPOOL grid, it had to demonstrate that the power it produced could be delivered anywhere in New England even while all other generators were running. This rule meant that there would be a strong New England grid with alternate transmission paths. Utilities in other regions sneered that New England was "over-built." But its rules, coupled with its relatively few interconnected lines with other states or Canadian provinces, meant that New England, harshly affected by the blackout of 1965, would be largely immune from what happened in 2003.

Whodunnit?

The attempts to find ready excuses would not suffice. Because of the international blame game and obvious public concern, the U.S. and Canadian governments agreed that a joint investigation was called for. Such an inquiry, like most government investigations contrived in times of crisis, would give the appearance of decisive action without assigning blame until most people had forgotten about the problem, and it would blunt the cross-border sniping.

Without needing an extensive investigation, the utility industry had determined in just a few days that at least one line had gone out on the grid of FirstEnergy Corp., headquartered in Akron, Ohio, and this outage was probably the start of the blackout. A line goes out of service because it is called upon to carry more electricity than is physically possible, and the outage is the same as a circuit breaker tripping or a fuse blowing and cutting off power when there is a short circuit in a person's home. If a power line carries more electricity than it should, it gets hot and sags. It could even break or start a fire. In either a person's home or on a utility system, when the line begins to carry more power than it should, the circuit is interrupted to prevent something worse from happening. The basic legal and practical requirements for electric service are that it be safe and reliable. Failing to meet these goals, a utility needs new management, and a homeowner needs a licensed electrician.

Right from the start, FirstEnergy had been identified as the probable cause of the blackout. But H. Peter Burg, FirstEnergy's chief executive officer, denied that any single event on his system could have been the origin of the cascading catastrophe. An Ohio newspaper claimed that the Bush administration would not focus on FirstEnergy because Burg, who soon after became fatally ill with cancer, was a major backer of the 2000 Bush-Cheney campaign. The company's political action committee had given Republicans almost $100,000 that year.

The international investigation went ahead, employing scores of people in both affected countries. It ultimately revealed that the FirstEnergy had badly bungled, and that the regional entity responsible for monitoring the Ohio company's behavior was almost literally asleep at the switch. The American and Canadian investigators uncovered the entire chain of events.[39]

At 1:31 P.M. on that August afternoon, about two and a half hours before the blackout began, an Ohio generator important to the safe operation of the transmission system shut down. That generator, known as Eastlake 5, would not cause the blackout by itself, but its absence would later allow the outage to happen. Next, on the neighboring system of Dayton Power & Light, a line tripped off because it had come in contact with a tree. Such a contact carries power through the tree into the ground rather than along the line, and in such cases the line automatically shuts down to avoid starting a fire. This outage would not cause the blackout either, but it made it more likely.

The Midwest Independent System Operator (MISO), an organization responsible for making sure the transmission grid is safe and reliable, had itself suffered the breakdown of a key piece of monitoring equipment and had no way of knowing that the situation on the grid was deteriorating. An operator there asked FirstEnergy why it had not dealt with a line that apparently went out of service. "We have no clue. Our computer is giving us fits, too,"[40] came the response. In fact, MISO personnel seemed unaware that they had no way of knowing what was happening and that they relied entirely on FirstEnergy for "real-time" information. All the FirstEnergy operator could tell MISO was: "I've got to get my calculator." On such flimsy monitoring the fate of millions depended. If MISO had known about the two problems that had cropped up, it could have taken emergency action. Like FirstEnergy, it did nothing.

MISO is a creation of the restructured world and reflects FERC's push for utilities to merge the control of their systems into larger units to facilitate larger markets. In principle, the plan is reasonable and perhaps desirable, but it was undoubtedly pushed faster than operators could handle. Utilities may have thought that the creation of larger transmission management entities was easier than it turned out to be. Whatever the reason, FERC had faith in MISO, and MISO was not ready.

On August 14, matters began to get worse. At 2:14 P.M., FirstEnergy's own alarm system failed, so operators would not be alerted to problems on its grid. By 2:54, the utility's computers were down, and staff had to be summoned to repair them. Then, between 3:05 and 3:41, three major power lines failed. As more power was diverted over them, they became overloaded, and each one came in contact with a tree that had been allowed to grow too tall. Power went onto the reduced number of remaining lines. FirstEnergy system operators did not know what was happening.

Why did so many lines come in contact with trees on the same afternoon? Trees grow in the spring and summer, and some had extended close to power lines. They had not been trimmed by the utility. When power lines carry increased amounts of electricity, they become hot and sag. If there is a strong wind, it may cool the lines, but on August 14, the wind dropped to less than two knots, and lines were failing, causing increased loads on the remaining lines. With each outage, the remaining lines sagged even more, and all the while, the operators knew nothing.

Why hadn't FirstEnergy trimmed the trees before they grew too close to the line? Utilities with approved rates may choose to reduce certain operating costs in order to boost profit margins. One of the first casualties in this cost cutting is tree trimming. Keeping trees away from wires may not be urgent under the right weather and operating conditions, and tree trimming usually suffers as the utility gambles that it can squeeze out more time before it must trim tree limbs. This gamble did not pay off for FirstEnergy.

Like water in a plumbing system, electrons will seek an alternate path if their "pipeline" is blocked because a power line is out of service. These electrons may flow onto another available power line to the point that it, too, becomes overloaded. It shuts down, and the electrons flow elsewhere, tripping lines as they go. This is called a "cascade." It had begun to happen on the grid.

Both neighboring transmission systems and generators connected to the FirstEnergy grid began to sense that something was wrong before the utility's own system operators did. As early as 2:32 P.M., they started calling FirstEnergy to report problems. Initially, FirstEnergy operators, not seeing problems on their own monitoring equipment, ignored the warnings. By 3:35 P.M., they recognized that there was a problem somewhere, but did not believe it was on their system. Just seven minutes later, as the grid moved toward a blackout, the operators began to understand that their monitoring equipment had failed. By 3:45 P.M., the operating staff reported that the utility was losing its transmission system. Even then, management failed to declare an emergency. After a series of increasingly urgent calls to its operators, FirstEnergy should have known by 3:56 P.M. that it faced a huge problem.

If it had acted according to usual utility practice, FirstEnergy would have begun cutting off service to customers, especially the larger ones, when it saw that lines were going out of service. Reducing demand for electricity is known as "load shedding," and it is a standard emergency measure, especially when customers want more power than can be produced or delivered to them at the moment. Normally the electric system operates to insure that there is always enough power being generated to meet customer demand. When you turn on even one light switch, an electric generator somewhere begins running faster, and power is delivered over the lines to the lightbulb. Similarly, if you turn off the light, a generator slows down. Turn off enough lights, and a generator can shut down.

On this August afternoon, there was enough power being generated to serve all customers, but there was not enough capacity on the wires to get it to them. As more electricity passed over fewer wires, FirstEnergy could have relieved the situation. By cutting customer purchases, it would have sent a signal to generators to slow down or shut off. This is the quickest way to solve problems on the electric system, and most utility companies can almost immediately dump their largest customers, such as factories and smelters.

The FirstEnergy operators thought that their monitoring system was the problem or that perhaps something was going wrong on a neighboring grid. Because they denied the possibility that the problem was on their own wires, the operators failed to declare an emergency or take any emergency action. All that other companies and generator operators on their own system could tell them in their many phone calls was that something was seriously wrong. The calls were not enough to prompt emergency action, mostly because FirstEnergy did not want to think the unthinkable.

As the clock climbed toward 4 P.M., more lines tripped out to avoid being overloaded. Akron and Cleveland went dark. Seventeen lines tripped, and only a couple could be restored to service. One of the lines that cut off was a 345,000 volt line (household current is about 110 volts) called Sammis-Star, and when it went off just before 4:06 PM, the cascade across the northeastern corner of the North American continent began. The problem was now well beyond the ability of FirstEnergy to solve, even had its operators understood what was happening.

FirstEnergy should have done better. It is the fifth-largest investor-owned utility in the United States, serving 4.4 million customers in Ohio, Pennsylvania, and New Jersey. At that size, it should have had the technical ability to detect and deal with the crisis in its early stages. Although it was the operators who failed, the responsibility fell on the executives who had underfunded tree trimming, had inadequately supervised the emergency response system, and had not provided the financial support necessary for training and equipment. Not one of FirstEnergy's top management would lose his job because of this failure. No regulator or politician would demand that anybody in management resign.

What happened next throughout the Northeast was a cascade much like what had already happened in Ohio that day and what had happened in 1965. When power from generators in Tennessee, Kentucky, and Missouri could no longer move across the shut FirstEnergy grid, it sought other routes, causing more lines to overload and trip off. Only then did the first major automatic event take place: the northeastern portion of the continent was separated from the rest of the North American grid. The Northeast was now, in terms of power supply, a large island.

On this huge, isolated grid, customers wanted more power than was available now that imports from outside the region were no longer being delivered. This was a somewhat different problem from what happened first, when the power supply was adequate but the power lines failed. But the solution would be much the same: a combination of dropping customers, taking lines out of service, and shutting down generators. Once a new balance was struck, the system could be gradually restored. Some pockets of the Northeast "island" had enough local generation to meet local demand, and power was quickly restored or never cut off. One of these "pockets" was most of New England.

About 50 million people were affected as the blackout cascaded through Ohio, Michigan, Pennsylvania, New York, New Jersey, Ontario, and small areas of Vermont, Massachusetts, and Connecticut. Some 61,800 megawatts (a large generator may supply 800 to 1,000 megawatts and a home may require 30 kilowatts a day) of customer demand had been cut off.

The U.S.-Canada joint investigation confirmed the direct causes of the blackout that were already known. They found four clear causes of the blackout of 2003. FirstEnergy did not understand its own system. It was not aware of what was happening on August 14. It did not manage tree growth on its transmission rights of way. And no entity responsible for the reliability of the grid kept track of what was happening as it occurred.

The utility had persistently failed to study its own system to find weaknesses or potentially extreme problems. It interpreted voluntary planning and operation standards in ways that were inadequate to keep the voltage up when there was a problem. Either it was incompetent or it simply kept its head in the sand.

Even after problems began to appear, FirstEnergy had "inadequate situational awareness" of what was happening, according to the investigators. Operators had no idea that their controls were not working, and if they had known, might not have known what to do. They could not test their equipment after repairs were made and did not have backup tools.

But everything kept coming back to FirstEnergy's failure to trim trees. This most simple of failures could have made the difference. Had those trees been trimmed, it is likely that the blackout of 2003 would never have taken place.

FirstEnergy does not exist in isolation. Lack of "real-time" data put MISO well below the standards that FERC thought that MISO was observing but had never checked. And MISO had no ability to act jointly with the neighboring reliability manager to deal with problems spotted in one another's area.

The blackout of 2003 began with a series of failures and inefficiencies that had nothing to do with the amount of transmission or the age of transmission lines. It resulted from the industry not taking responsibility for managing the grid with the kind of care that would reflect the dependence of millions of people on its operation.

During the day on August 15, most areas regained power, and life returned to normal. In some spots, the outage lasted a week. What could have been a nightmare was this time only a bad dream, although the governor of Michigan claimed that the economy of her state had suffered a $1 billion blow.

Transmission off the Track

The blackout of 2003 should not have happened. That it did happen reveals that more was wrong than the incompetence of the FirstEnergy operators. The electric industry and the government that regulates it had failed to meet their basic responsibilities. They had no excuse; they had been warned.

The U.S.-Canada investigators found that the 2003 outage shared many characteristics with earlier blackouts. Poor tree trimming, "failure to ensure operation within secure limits" and "inadequate operator training." were common causes of blackouts Two years after the blackout, on September 12, 2005, a blackout hit more than 2 million people in Los Angeles. The cause was obvious operator error; a worker had cut a line, causing a cascade on the municipal utility system. Forty years after the major Northeast blackout of

1965, utilities continued to make the same kind of mistakes that caused many other outages in the intervening years.

FirstEnergy (along with many other utilities) was not ready for a crisis that could lead to a blackout. It barely observed NERC guidelines, and its intent was clearly to do as little as possible to achieve NERC goals. The Ohio company's personnel were poorly trained and insensitive to the signals they received, but what FirstEnergy lacked above all was oversight. Neither the company nor the regional reliability organization to which it belonged was ready to track on a "real-time" basis what was taking place. NERC or one of its regional groups would look at problems only after they happened.

Regulators played no role at all. If a utility chose to apply NERC guidelines vigorously, it had a good chance of avoiding major problems. If it chose to save money and enhance profits, nobody cared or was even aware of what it was doing until there was a blackout. Essentially, the system itself was not reliable and was based on trusting to luck. The blackout of 2003 was born of a combination of incompetence, complacency, and greed.

Government had essentially ignored the 1965 warning and did not try to force FirstEnergy or any other utility to take preventive action to reduce the chance of blackouts. Under the Commerce Clause of the U.S. Constitution, transmission is subject to federal jurisdiction because it involves interstate commerce. But in the face of the utility campaign against FPC legislation, federal regulators made no attempt even to increase their own staff's competence. State utility regulators, usually eager to keep control away from the FPC or FERC, did no better. Regulation of transmission at both federal and state levels was limited to a cursory review of the costs included in a utility's revenue requirement.

Transmission costs have never been a major issue for regulators because they are only about 10 percent of the total cost of power delivered to a customer. The low priority given to transmission in setting utility rates, excessive confidence in the ability of utilities to deal with technical problems, or simple indifference caused regulators to neglect the grid. Before 1965, there was no Department of Energy, and the Johnson administration preferred to rely on the industry's promises of good behavior rather than seeking more government regulation.

Even after the blackout of 1965, the very nature of government regulation of utilities at both the federal and state levels encouraged the utility companies to do as little as possible to remedy problems that could lead to blackouts. Before industry restructuring in the 1990s, the purpose of regulation was to provide a substitute for competition. But by focusing on rates alone, regulation provided what economists call a "perverse incentive." Companies were supposed to provide safe and reliable service but could increase their profits by quietly cutting their expenses to the bone. The net result was to discourage utilities to take any action that would not guarantee a better profit margin. This kind of regulatory regime works only until the lights go out.

The second huge blackout in thirty-eight years proved that something had gone wrong—or rather that nothing had gone right. NERC standards lacked any enforcement authority, allowing FirstEnergy to be unprepared to deal with a single major outage. And the lack of sufficient transmission lines to insure reliability was the biggest failure of the industry and the regulators.

Electric industry restructuring contributed to the 2003 grid fiasco. Generators began to appear at environmentally acceptable places on the grid, but the high-voltage lines linking these sites with concentrations of customers were often inadequate. Restructuring gave license to generators to site wherever they wanted and though transmission owners were required to build new lines when the existing grid was insufficient, the new rules lacked force and urgency. Regulators seemed to believe that the problems would sort themselves out in due course; they shifted their focus to creating market rules.

EPAct was interpreted to mean that the market would be the ultimate regulator. That might work in setting the price of generation and allocating the risk attached to building new plants, but nobody paid any attention to insuring that transmission—still a monopoly not subject to market forces—would be adequate or any more reliable than in the past.

After issuing Order 888, FERC apparently believed that its requirement that transmission owners would have to build more lines if generators needed them would take care of the reliability problem. It established a detailed description of the process for getting new lines built, making it possible that all cost would be paid by the new generators. The new rules required that the generation companies pay for studies to see if the existing grid was adequate or if new lines would be needed when a new generator was planned. It was presumed that a company would refrain from building a generating plant if the transmission costs turned out to be too high.

In some parts of the country—and especially in the Northeast— the result of this new system was a free-for-all as investors sought to grab the best sites to avoid building new transmission lines. Some gambled on the belief that there would be more capacity on the grid in practice than had been previously thought, or that the rules would change and others would pay for grid upgrades, or that reliability standards would be lowered so that nobody would have to pay for upgrades.

The federal regulators also seemed to assume that state siting authorities could readily overcome environmental objections to constructing the new lines. Beyond all of the uncertainty unleashed by the new rules of the game, the problem of facility siting, a matter under the jurisdiction of the states, had been underrated. The open market, which allowed a generator to be sited wherever its owners wanted, would inevitably require new transmission lines at some time. States might make it relatively easy for generators to be built, but environmental opposition could make it much more difficult, especially when new transmission was necessary, and such opposition put the entire industry restructuring in jeopardy.

Energy facility siting was growing more costly and complicated, particularly in the Northeast, where high generation costs spurred great interest in having new generators to compete with or replace the old. Many people did not like the looks of huge transmission towers or swaths of land newly cleared of trees to provide a path for power lines or worried about the electromagnetic fields around high-voltage lines. There was little consideration of how increasingly inadequate lines could serve growing needs and no proof that electromagnetic fields did any harm, but opponents raised serious obstacles to building new lines.

Many generation owners, promoters of the open market, complained indirectly that environmental interests, the despised "tree huggers," were preventing construction of the new power lines needed to facilitate both new power supply and lower prices through competition. The blackout of 2003 gave them a lever to try to loosen environmental controls and get more transmission built. That would be a high price to pay for the ineptitude displayed in Akron.

FERC had begun to apply EPAct in the belief that the transmission owners would readily allow their transmission wires to be run as common carriers by independent operators and would even be willing to sell them to independent owners. But it had chosen to shift its focus from transmission access to market rules. Market makers started calling the regulatory shots, and transmission policy suffered.

The Case of Curt Hébert

Nowhere was that more apparent than in the case of FERC chairman Curt Hébert, a protégé of then Senate Majority Leader Trent Lott. Hébert understood the need to press hard to promote the concept of owner-operators of the grid whose sole interest was running an essential service for profit. Only if the grid were run independently of generation-owning utilities and with incentives to be reliable and truly open, Hébert reasoned, could a market be established that would be open to all who wanted to develop generators.

Two events intervened to block Hébert's vision. First, George W. Bush was elected president of the United States. Second, Trent Lott lost his clout and his position as majority leader when a Vermont GOP senator defected, becoming an independent and siding with the Democrats, giving them Senate control. Without Lott's help, Hébert depended entirely on the Bush White House to keep him in his job.

A few months into Bush's term, Hébert received a call from Enron chief Ken Lay. "Kenny Boy," as his friend Bush called him, told Hébert that he would lend his support at the White House for his renomination to FERC provided the regulator cooperated with Enron's ideas for market design and supported more aggressive market rules. Hébert was ambitious but he was also a serious regulator, having previously served as the chairman of the Mississippi regulatory commission. Not only did he balk at Lay's suggestion, he went public with the details of the conversation. In one of the rare times when a utility story is big news, Lay's offer to Hébert made the front page of *The New York Times*.[41] Hébert obviously resented any implication that he would trade his independent judgment for political reward. Politically, going public would at least delay any action Bush could take to replace him, because the president would not want to look as though he was giving Lay what he wanted, at least not right away. But Hébert was doomed.

Not only was Hébert denied reappointment, but Bush chose Pat Wood, the head of his own Texas Public Utility Commission, to become FERC chairman. In an oddity of transmission geography, most of Texas transmission is not subject to federal control, a status shared only by Alaska and Hawaii. Power from these two noncontiguous states cannot be included in interstate commerce, but the federal government has arbitrarily determined that Texas is also not connected to the national grid. Not surprisingly, Wood had shown little interest in the issues Hébert had raised and much interest in the needs of Enron, a Texas-based corporation. Even more important, Wood seemed intent on nonutility grid operation by ISOs, which was strongly supported by Enron. This proposal meant that no new transmission would be built, because ISOs have no vested interest in new power lines and, as nonprofits, no incentive to build. This policy ran directly counter to Hébert's.

Under the Bush administration team at FERC, the adoption of congestion pricing, a policy designed to delay the need for new transmission lines, served to weaken the ability of the grid to serve all generators. By delaying as long as possible the construction of new transmission lines, FERC wanted to squeeze every bit of service out of existing lines. This policy does nothing to promote reliability or reduce bottlenecks. While it avoids overbuilding and may save customers expense, it is intended to push power lines to the limits of their reliability.

The commission also undermined the NEPOOL principle that

before a new generator could be hooked to the grid, it had to show that it could serve anybody on the grid without degrading any existing service. Generators, eager to get into business, claimed that they did not want to serve customers anywhere on the grid—just those who could be reached without causing any overloads. This policy makes for good economics (for the generators, at least) but bad physics. Once the electrons enter the transmission system, they do not "know" who is buying them. They simply flow wherever they can, which may result in reduced reliability. That can be a high price to pay for the sake of increased competition.

After effectively eliminating NEPOOL's rule requiring new generators to insure grid reliability, FERC virtually abolished NEPOOL itself, preferring to impose its own rules, which had not performed well, instead of the NEPOOL system that had functioned successfully since 1972.

Yet another reason new transmission lines have not been constructed is that FERC has had a difficult time deciding who should pay for them. Developers want to avoid bearing the cost and claim that all users should shoulder the cost of any upgrades or expansions because, they say, everybody benefits from an increase in grid reliability. Customers, represented by state regulators, want developers to pay costs that would not have been incurred but for their connecting to the grid. This has become known as the "but for" principle. It has taken FERC years to settle the debate even partly, and meanwhile developers have looked for ways to get onto the grid without having to pay. The confusion not only has deterred generator developers, whose success is essential to a restructured industry, but, because nobody wants to pay for new transmission, has reduced grid reliability.

Electric companies grew up locally and spread to larger interconnected areas, creating gaps between them that remain in many areas, especially those with less population density. In the Mid-Atlantic area systems are strongly interconnected, and if one fails, it can take others down with it. By contrast, in the West, where lightly populated areas serve as buffers between utility companies, problems are less readily passed from one system to the next. It is not an accident that most major blackouts unrelated to nature have taken place in the Northeast, with almost nothing comparable having taken place elsewhere on the continent.

New England was spared the blackout of 2003 not only because of the strength of its own transmission system, a vestige of the old NEPOOL rules, but also because of the lack of many major inter-connections with the rest of the grid. Though FERC had tried to force New England and New York to use a single transmission man-ager, the two sides could never agree. Isolation turned out to be New England's good fortune and made a good case for resisting the FERC plans for a national market.

FERC has pushed for either a national grid system or no more than a handful of huge regions but had failed because of utility opposition. The most that FERC had been able to accomplish in some areas is more centralized management of the grid. MISO, responsible for the region in which FirstEnergy is located, is one of these new managers. Because it did not impose any mandatory operating criteria, FERC has made it possible for fewer people to make bigger mistakes.

The blackout of 2003 revealed that the grid was as vulnerable as it had ever been. The regulators had made the situation even worse by pursuing abstract market principles without paying enough attention to the effects of their actions on grid reliability. Contin-uing to insist that the utilities were responsible for maintaining reli-ability was unrealistic.

Fixing It

The events of August 14, 2003, could not be ignored, and Congress came under mounting public pressure to insure a reliable power supply. "We simply cannot afford to wait any longer,"[42] said Representative Billy Tauzin, then–GOP energy leader in the U.S. House of Representatives. Republicans wasted no time in trying to exploit public concern about blackouts to gain their objectives in federal energy legislation, which had languished before Congress for years. They gave the first priority to supporting demands by southern and western utilities to prevent FERC from imposing rules that could create larger electric markets.

Large utilities such as the Atlanta-based Southern Company have successfully impeded the growth of a competitive market in these regions and have convinced their state government officials that old-fashioned utility monopolies work better than the restructured industry. They do not want to be forced into larger markets that could challenge their local dominance. The GOP, with a strong base in the same states of the South and West that have resisted the coming of competition, sought to ban not only FERC's plans for larger market areas but any serious attempt to put transmission, the supposed common carrier, under management independent of the utilities.

By the end of 2003, the principal focus of the energy bill had reverted to providing billions of dollars in tax breaks to the generators and a big handout to ethanol developers, abolishing PUHCA, as the utilities had proposed, and providing special liability protection for companies that had used the gasoline additive MTBE. Fixing grid reliability had become a mere footnote.

Meanwhile, FERC and NERC, rivals if not evil twins, found themselves trying to come up with solutions to the blackout problem. A turf battle threatened, especially when NERC, not subject to regulatory oversight because it was a utility trade organization with no real powers, laid out plans to transform itself into something like a transmission regulator and even to get itself formally recognized. NERC was slated to become the North American Electric Reliability Organization, although it did not push the ominous acronym NERO for long. Its directors would be independent of utility control from now on, and it would develop tougher standards. To make these standards stick, it would need the imprimatur of the federal government.

None of this made FERC happy. Still the absolute, if ineffectual, regulator of transmission, FERC felt that NERC was proposing to take over authority for insuring reliability in the future. But for the time being, at least, FERC lacked sufficient legislative authority to take actions such as those proposed by NERC. It had been forced to search its regulatory cupboard for whatever authority it might have over transmission operations and to cooperate with the still-independent NERC.

In April 2004, the U.S.-Canada blackout investigators issued their final report. To nobody's surprise, the first of their forty-six recommendations stated: "Make reliability standards mandatory and enforceable, with penalties for noncompliance." Not one recommendation dealt with any supposed inadequacy or antiquity of the grid. While the transmission grid might need upgrading, enforceable operating standards were the first requirement. The only equipment recommendations called for more and better IT equipment. But the final report recognized that NERC, from the industry itself, had come up with proposals for dealing with blackouts, while Congress had not. Because of this, the report suggested that the ERO (the "N" had been dropped), sure to be the former NERC, should handle reliability matters under FERC, which would have the ultimate power of approval or disapproval of proposed standards.

Congress, meanwhile, had done nothing useful. The Republicans banned the Democrats from negotiations on the energy bill and hammered out their own legislation. After failing to pass a bill at the end of 2003 because the MTBE bailout was unacceptable even to some Republicans, the GOP leaders focused transmission discussions on ways to get more tax breaks to grid owners, a provision consistent with the character of the bill as an aid-to-industry measure.

Frozen out of the energy bill discussions, the Democrats came up with a much less complex bill called the Electric Reliability Act of 2004. Clearly an attempt to embarrass the Republicans, the bill would give FERC the authority to put into effect the U.S.-Canada investigation recommendations for FERC and the ERO, including giving FERC the power to impose penalties for noncompliance. But the Republican leadership in Congress opposed this legislation, clinging to their belief that only a comprehensive energy bill would work and, presumably, that concern about electric transmission reliability could be used to reward the industry itself. With this strategy, measures to avert blackouts were held hostage to the special interests seeking federal tax breaks and other targeted benefits.

Finally, in 2005, almost two years after the blackout, Congress passed an energy bill. Perhaps in honor of the first President Bush's legislation, it was called the Energy Policy Act of 2005.[43] The new law included a section called the Electricity Modernization Act of 2005, which repealed PUHCA, gutted PURPA, and finally placed transmission reliability under mandatory regulation.

The 2005 legislation followed the U.S.-Canada commission recommendations calling for an ERO "to establish and enforce reliability standards for the bulk-power system, subject to [FERC] Commission review." FERC will set the goals for the ERO to reach. The ERO will have the authority to impose unspecified penalties on entities not following its rules, subject to appeal to FERC. It may also delegate its power to regional bodies, suggesting that its existing reliability councils will exercise effective control. It remains to be seen if major utilities can dominate their regional reliability councils, creating the potential for a test of federal control.

Before the 2005 legislation, FERC could override state and local objections to the construction of interstate natural gas pipelines but had no such authority for electricity. The passage of natural gas through pipelines occurs in interstate commerce, and because the U.S. Constitution provides that federal law supercedes state laws on the same matters, the Natural Gas Act allowed for the construction of new access to natural gas supply. The Federal Power Act contained no such provision, at best giving FERC jurisdiction coordinated with the states but denying a federal right of eminent domain. The 2005 electricity law remedies this gap in federal jurisdiction. For the first time, there is a statement of national policy that the United States' need for more transmission can be ranked higher than other interests. The law also provides authority for funding new transmission technologies and for allowing incentive rates for transmission providers. These provisions may get more transmission built, but they may have little effect on the grid already under the control of its owners. Finally, the law allows FERC to pass the costs of transmission upgrades to entities that have caused the need for the upgrade.

While much depends on the effects of these measures—effects that are currently unclear, given the history of opposition by the major utilities to some of the fundamental changes intended to result from industry restructuring—any success will not come quickly. The 2005 law calls for accelerated FERC rule-making, but sorting out the role of the ERO, making sure that its standards are effective and enforceable, and clearing the way for new transmission will take years.

Consumers have a glimmer of hope. New transmission can be financed by private transmission-owning companies or by generators connecting to the grid and not by customers. Yet subsidies to generators, forced on customers by system operators, may offset such gains. Customers will also pay for incentives for new transmission. Transmission reliability should come to depend increasingly on the expertise of engineers rather than on utility executives more intent on diverting funds to the bottom line than in assuring reliability. New lines should be constructed where needed and not be the victim of environmental opponents who want their lights to come on at the flip of a switch yet refuse to make any sacrifices to make that possible.

It may be difficult for the American consumer to grasp fully the changes that have been taking place in a restructured electric industry. But everyone understands a blackout when it happens. Blackouts have been rare, occasionally catastrophic events, but they send a clear message about the vulnerability of electric service. While some in the industry have recognized the need for more regulation of the grid and not just for more money for new lines, Congress has delayed while it responded to the challenge of the 2003 blackout and at the same time met the demands of well-heeled constituents more eager for a handout than a solution.

If the 2005 law results primarily in the construction of new lines and not in the imposition of binding operational standards, the message of the blackout of 2003 will have been missed. Yet that might happen. In the wake of Hurricane Katrina in 2005, former FERC chair Pat Wood said that the reason for outages on the Entergy system in Louisiana was the utility's underfunding of new transmission. Entergy disagreed. Nobody talked about grid management, and nobody would say that there are simply times when nature will force the lights to go out.

Consumers expect that the electric system will be reliable, especially because it has become so essential to their lives. More than 120 years after the first wires carried power from a central station, the industry still fails to meet this test.

Unless and until FERC gives transmission reliability and control as high a priority as complex market rules, another major blackout is virtually inevitable. It may come soon, and it will be bad.

CHAPTER 7

THE GHOST OF SAM INSULL:
THE RETURN OF THE MEGACOMPANIES

The new pattern of the electric industry has emerged: it is a comeback for Sam Insull. The electric business is increasingly dominated by a handful of giant multistate corporations.

Taking advantage of the new opportunities—and in fact promoting them—was Exelon Corp. Originally Commonwealth Edison of Chicago, the company from which Insull had launched his empire, Exelon was becoming a multistate force. It acquired PECO Energy, the Philadelphia-based utility, and in 2005 moved to purchase Public Service Enterprise Group of New Jersey. Its operations would spread across the MISO and PJM markets.

Other utilities and consumer groups worried that Exelon would end up with too much market power. Though it had divested itself of generation in Illinois, it continued to buy and sell power on a massive scale, including some from generators it owned elsewhere, causing customers to worry that its market dominance could allow it to set prices artificially high. "I have to convince other people that the market will work,"[44] said John Rowe, the Exelon chief. At the same time, utilities feared that Exelon could dominate the use of the transmission grid over a wide area, essentially limiting their options and setting prices that could render some of their assets virtually worthless. "Utilities Fear Power of Supercharged Exelon,"[45] read the headlines, as the battle emerged into public view.

Nothing in Exelon's brief history or Rowe's career suggested that the company would behave like Enron or, for that matter, Insull. But its sheer size was somewhat chilling proof that industry restructuring would mean the end of many smaller utilities, which had been easier to keep under some degree of regulatory control. FERC, which itself had failed to perceive what was happening in California, was the cheerleader for such change.

The growth of Exelon was likely to be paralleled by other mergers. For example, North Carolina–based Duke Energy, one of the nation's largest utilities and a California games player, moved to take over Cinergy, a large Midwest company. The merged company would have operations in five states. The Mid-American Energy acquisition of Pacificorp would give it operations in twelve states, six in the West and six in the Midwest. The FPL merger with Constellation Energy would create a dominant entity along the East Coast from Maine to Florida.

PUHCA Repealed

A funny thing happened on the way to fewer and bigger power companies. In May 2005, an administrative law judge at the SEC ruled that a merger in 2000 between American Electric Power, a major company in the Midwest, and Central & South West, an Oklahoma-Texas-Louisiana utility, violated PUHCA. The SEC had initially approved the merger but had been ordered by a federal court to reconsider because it had ignored PUHCA's merger restrictions, which stated that the operating companies under a single holding company had to be located in contiguous regions. In the new decision, the judge found that the combined service area was not a single integrated region. The SEC had gone along with the changing times and approved the merger because it had begun winking at PUHCA requirements. But after the court's chastisement, the SEC judge could not ignore the legitimate and obvious consumer complaints that PUHCA was being violated.

The decision was soon made meaningless, however, because the new piece of energy legislation, just two months away, would include the repeal of PUHCA. The utilities had at last convinced Congress that the protection offered by PUHCA was no longer necessary, mostly because it was no longer relevant: EPAct had authorized utilities to own generators, deregulated since the 1992 law, anywhere in the country while enjoying an exemption from PUHCA. The utilities argued that it was anachronistic to regulate holding companies and limit their ability to own companies in other parts of the country, when generators were no longer subject to such restrictions. Only a few voices representing consumer interests fought until the end against repeal, opposing the elimination of the many consumer protections that were also an integral part of the law.

The utilities improved the deal they had made when the 1992 EPAct had passed. While they must provide open transmission access to others in return for gaining the right to compete in other markets, they can now own utilities as well as generators anywhere in the country. The investor-owned utilities had also argued that PUHCA was no longer needed because there would be enough healthy competitors to insure that the market itself regulated behavior. "PUHCA is an outmoded statute that imposes barriers to

competition and discourages investment in generation and transmission,"[46] said New Mexico Republican Senator Pete Domenici,
chairman of the Senate Energy Committee. "PUHCA's investment
restrictions and physical integration requirements are no longer
practical. PUHCA limits geographic and product diversification and
imposes many burdensome filing requirements."

What about the consumer? "Repealing PUHCA does not mean
the repeal of consumer protections," Domenici said. "State and federal regulators will be able to continue to protect ratepayers as they
did before PUHCA repeal." Continue what protection? The states
had not been required or even allowed to protect consumers against
the actions of monoliths that had been banned under federal law.
The SEC had exercised federal authority but will do so no longer.
FERC now has complete control over the market power of the
enlarged national power companies, including efforts to manipulate
the market. This is the same agency that disastrously denied the existence of the California energy crisis.

A dozen years after electric industry restructuring was launched,
what had changed? Generation had mostly been separated from the
rest of the utility business. A plethora of new players had emerged
and then been consolidated or acquired by large utility companies.
These companies owned generators, transmission and distribution
companies, and marketers. They had strong holds on their customers.
The structure did not look radically different from the period before
1992 or even before 1978, when PURPA was enacted. If there was any
appreciable change, it was that the largest utilities now dominated to
an even greater extent and with fewer legal restrictions.

Take the Southern Company, headquartered in Atlanta. If you
read its Annual Report, you could easily believe that nothing much
has happened to the utility industry since the heyday of Sam Insull.
You would not find any mention of wholesale competition, because

there is no sign that any independent, nonutility supplier has ever been able to sell electricity to a single Southern customer. Back in the fine print—the notes to the financial reports—you might notice, however, that federal regulators had been trying to get the Southern Company to turn control of its transmission system over to an independent body.

Electric industry restructuring, designed to provide customers with greater choice through competition, simply has not arrived for the Southern Company or most of the United States. Utilities in the South and West, where power supply costs have not climbed as high as in the Northeast and in California, have done their best to ignore change and induce government to leave them alone. They have met with remarkable success, partly because of their political clout and partly because of the comparative failure of the competitive model.

One reason why the electric rates in some states are comparatively low is that these states resisted the application of PURPA. Utilities in these states refrained from purchasing power from outside suppliers. In states where PURPA was applied aggressively, the notion of long-term avoided cost, the price to be paid for power based on renewable resources, meant going beyond the current price of power from traditional sources. If you forecast power supply costs based on expectations of higher fuel bills, more a matter of conjecture than knowledge, you could come up with sufficiently high avoided costs to encourage renewable resource–based generators to enter the business and force utilities to buy from them. But if you focused only on short-term avoided cost—today's cost—you could prevent high-cost PURPA contracts. Most states did just that.

States in the South and West often benefited from lower-cost power supply because of the influence of taxpayer-subsidized federal power administrations. In addition, thanks to less stringent environmental regulation by both some states and the federal government, some states relied heavily on high-emission, coal-fired generators. Such factors brought lower current costs and the ability to bypass the intentions of PURPA power. In effect, the federal government was pursuing contradictory policies. High-price states saw prices rise even higher, and the others held the line with good rates. Not surprisingly, customers in low-cost states did not protest against PURPA, as some did in the North. They did not even know about it.

In the low-cost states, traditional utility regulation continued almost unchanged. Take, for example, Georgia Power, one of the utilities owned by the Southern Company. In 2004, the Georgia utility regulators approved a rate increase (Georgia Power calls it a "rate plan") of more than $200 million. This increase did not include increases in fuel costs, which the power company would seek to recover through another rate increase. The new rates included an after-tax return on investment in a range of 10.25 percent to 12.25 percent. Only if the return climbed above the ceiling would Georgia Power have to give two thirds of the excess to its customers. Georgia Power is assured of this arrangement for at least three years, after which the regulator may determine if it wants to extend it. Meanwhile, the utility is protected from the kind of fluctuations in return that are characteristic of most other investments.

Contrast this return with historic returns in the stock market. The long-term return on investment of all stocks, including returns on those far riskier than utility shares and gains during the heady post–World War II decades, was about 7 percent after taxes. Why would a utility want to enter into the new world of competitive power if it could induce regulators to allow it to earn almost twice the historical average of companies not "benefiting" from the state regulation?

Traditional utilities operate under a cozy system of what is called "rate-of-return" or "cost-of-service" regulation. They try to convince state regulators that the costs they have incurred, usually in a recent one-year period, are normal and not wasteful or inflated. If they succeed, as they usually do, the utilities are entitled to recover these costs from their customers. To finance capital investment in generators and wires, utilities raise money from their shareholders and by borrowing. The return on the shareholders' equity investment is also allowed as part of the cost of service. While utilities are not guaranteed this return, they are given the ability to earn it. And if operating costs increase because of rising fuel prices or the effects of a hurricane, the regulators will allow utilities to increase their rates even more to recover those costs from their customers, thus greatly reducing risk for investors.

Other kinds of companies, faced with adverse conditions and relying on investment capital, have to trust their ability to get customers to pay higher prices if they are to earn expected returns. Because utilities have a reasonable chance to earn their promised return, they have traditionally been considered safe investments. Utility monopolies, which have managed to avoid competition, continue to enjoy safer returns. When those returns meet or exceed those of more speculative investments, the stock market deems a utility like Southern Company to be extremely successful.

Utilities Keep Control

In 1999, when FERC announced its policy of trying to get utilities to turn their transmission assets over to independent entities, the Southern Company took the possibility seriously and, like utilities across the country, considered how such a system might operate and what the value of its transmission assets might be if and when they were placed under the control of an independent entity. But Southern Company also undertook to make sure that day would never come.

Sales and Revenues 2003		
	Sales	Revenues
Investor-owned Utilities	62.4%	65.2%
Publicly owned Utilities	16.6%	15.8%
Power Marketers	10.3%	9.3%
Cooperatives	9.7%	9.3%
Federal Power Agencies	1.0%	0.4%
Source: American Public Power Association		

Dispatching its regulatory staff and lobbyists to talk with regulators and legislators in Washington and around the country, Southern Company and its allies fought hard to derail FERC's plans. As strong supporters of the Bush presidential bid in 2000, just after the FERC policy was announced, their efforts were rewarded, and they were able to put a stop to any initiative that would force them to give up any meaningful degree of control over their own transmission facilities. Usually politicians stay away from utility regulatory matters. In this case, members of Congress from Southern Company's states were said to be lobbying the White House and FERC commissioners in an effective effort to keep hands off their utility. Beyond the influence that Southern Company could wield, it was reasonable to argue that its rates could remain lower if it were left under traditional regulation and it would still reap handsome gains, a situation satisfactory to both customers and shareholders. Here was a company that was an apostle of free enterprise and open-market competition now arguing against the very measures designed to achieve its objectives and opting instead for full governmental regulation, if only at the state level.

FERC's objective was to insure that entities owning generation would not be able to operate their transmission systems to favor their own supply over power transmitted over their wires from unregulated entities. If the 1992 EPAct was to work, it would depend on the transmission lines being treated like common carriers. In other words, anybody who could pay the fare would be allowed to ride the bus, and there would be no discrimination among passengers concerning either access or cost.

But utilities that remained vertically integrated, with generation, transmission, and distribution remaining bundled, preferred to have a priority right to use their facilities to serve end-use customers on their systems. That preference could make it less expensive for them to serve their customers from their own generators rather than from independent sources, and those independent sources could find themselves paying more for transmission. That would effectively stifle competition. This situation could arise because the third-party users of the utility transmission lines could find that all existing lines were committed to serving the captive retail customers, known as the "native load." The newcomers would be required to bear the cost of upgrading the utility grid. That added cost would certainly discourage competition.

FERC recognized that favoring native load could frustrate the goals of the restructuring law. All power supply is destined to serve some end-use customer, it reasoned, so there was no plausible reason to discriminate in favor of the local utility's customers and, inevitably, against new players in the market. In the waning days of the Clinton administration, FERC had supported this position unanimously. As one FERC chairman had said earlier: "Everybody is somebody's native load."[47] The snickering that followed this remark was almost audible.

On this matter, the incumbent and still-bundled utilities prevailed. FERC, newly reconstituted by the Bush administration, leaned toward supporting the priority of use of the grid by its owner to serve the company's native load. By this action, FERC had acquiesced in the most minimal interpretation of the 1992 law. In the 2005 law, the matter was settled in favor of native-load priority.

In most states, there was no requirement to open the grid for the purposes of retail competition. A status quo policy meant that the states did not require unbundling of control over generation and transmission. Coupled with a FERC policy allowing preference for native load in the use of transmission, there was no real need to change the way business was done. Any change to meet federal requirements was little more than an illusion.

Despite their hostility toward change, at least as it affected them, the utilities enjoying virtually uninterrupted monopolies liked the prospect of playing in other people's yards. They would find it attractive to set up affiliates to enter into the business of selling power in states with competitive markets.

Generators and Their Owners

The EPAct drafters believed that the law would encourage investment in companies devoted entirely to generation. Because they could operate outside the regulatory sphere, such companies would enjoy great flexibility. With no utility involvement, utility customers would bear no risk of having to pay for generator investment, while the owners of the independent plants might well expect returns above those normally allowed under regulation.

At first, plans for new generators were announced at a blistering pace in some regions. In New England, for example, proposals were announced that equaled the existing generation capacity in the region. In theory, an open market including power sold at competitive prices would stimulate demand. Although the theory held that new generators would simply push out the old, many vintage units were worthy competitors. New England utilities and states had embraced unbundling and competition, so that region seemed particularly fertile. When utilities were required to divest themselves of their generators, independent companies stepped forward to buy them, often at inflated prices. Optimism was rampant.

What had seemed to be a lucrative business turned out to be excessively risky. The boom times created a glut. Merchant generation, as independent generation is known, would depend heavily on sales of power under contracts that are much shorter than was characteristic in the industry before restructuring. However, their debt financing had to be long-term. It was difficult to find lenders who would support this way of doing business. The Enron collapse, though it had little to do with the generating business, further worried lenders about supporting merchant generators, whose finances were uncertain. Furthermore, the rules that grew up around the competitive business and the limits on the physical availability of transmission lines made it evident that new generators could not exploit all market opportunities that might exist. In short, EPAct had been based on a superficial understanding of the way the market might develop and on relative ignorance about the difficulties of financing merchant generation. Investors came to realize that the new electric industry did not offer easy money from a captive market, but by the time they reached that realization, they had assumed a significant level of risk. Much of the investment turned sour, and the rush to enter the market slowed to a trickle. Major utilities bought many of the units, sometimes at bargain prices.

When the industry settled out, there was only a handful of merchant generating companies, those not affiliated with operating utilities. These included Mirant, the Southern Company spin-off fighting to emerge from bankruptcy, Calpine, also bankrupt, and AES, supposedly the lone success story, though it failed to issue a quarterly report in mid-2005 because it had to restate its financial results for the previous year.

Of the hundred largest owners of generators in the United States, only these three are significant independent players. The top ten include nine megautilities: American Electric Power, Southern Company, Exelon, Xcel Energy, Entergy, Duke, Progress Energy, and FPL Group. The only outsider in this leading group is the Tennessee Valley Authority. These nine own 34 percent of the generation output in the United States for utility purposes. AES comes in twenty-eighth.[48] The new model of the competitive market is not working.

Nowhere was that more evident than in Ohio and Michigan, both states that opted for retail access. On the grounds that generation was needed to insure reliability, state regulators favored allowing the old-line utilities to build new generators and pass the capital costs on to all customers, even those buying power generated by independent producers. This proposal, fought by independent generators, which had proliferated since the opening of market access, could undermine the market by favoring the established utilities and restoring to customers the risk of paying for failed or unnecessary generators.

The newly structured industry, even though utility-dominated, is not stable. In 2005, Duke decided to get out of the wholesale power and trading business and sell most of the generators, rated at 6,200 megawatts, it had developed to compete in markets such as California, Arizona, and the Northeast. Duke's CEO said that the collapse of the merchant industry caused by Enron had "shaken up" Duke.[49] "When everything collapsed, the company found itself with a business model that depended on factors that don't exist anymore," he said.

Power Marketers: Inevitable and in Trouble

If generators did not meet EPAct expectations, a new entity—the power marketer—came to symbolize the new, competitive world. If the power industry turned out to be anything like telecommunications, customers should see many companies reselling electricity from generators owned by others. In fact, the genius of the open market might be the ways in which marketers packaged their energy products. Perhaps they could be sold together with telephone service or home security—or even cable television. It seemed possible that anything connecting to the home or business by wire could be sold by marketers.

Reality was less attractive than this fantasy. Entrenched companies were not tempted to pool their products with others. Potential new marketers found it difficult to come up with the financing to assure generation owners that they could make good on their financial commitments to make payments based on customer sales. In fact, only Enron emerged as a major player that could claim to sell power without actually owning any, merely buying the rights to generator output in the open market. But Enron itself was a fantasy, and a pernicious one that harmed its customers and investors.

Marketers were essential in dealing with the demands of the new market. They became expert in dealing with customers and ISOs. Though they sometimes adopted attractive names, below the surface they almost always turned out to be fronts for operating utilities. In fact, some of the utilities changed their names to make themselves appear transformed to play in the market. For example, Virginia's Dominion Electric became Evantage, Cincinnati Electric became Cinergy, and Illinois Power became Illinova.

The major power companies thus became the major marketers, able to draw on their own resources while conducting a trading operation, which allowed them to purchase some supply in the open market. As the number of players—generators, wires companies, utilities—in the electric business declined, so did the number of marketers. And they sold only power, so the dream of an all-inclusive wires service was put off to another day.

While the arrival of marketers brought the prospect of competitive benefits, the underlying truth is that the major utilities—Duke, Exelon, Xcel, and the others—ended up as the dominant players. These players could easily determine the pace at which the market opened and the scope of the benefits customers might expect.

The case of Mirant Corp. is a classic tale of the failure of high hopes for the restructured market and of the role of the big utilities. Originally known as Southern Energy, it was formed in 1993, soon after the passage of EPAct, as a wholly owned subsidiary of Southern Company. It grew gradually into one of the major competitive energy companies, owning or leasing generation as well as running a trading desk. The CEO of Southern Company retired into a similar position with Mirant.

As some of the wildly optimistic promise of the competitive market waned for Mirant, just as it did for Enron, Southern Company began to become nervous about its commitment. In 2000, Mirant offered some stock to the public, although Southern Company retained dominant control. By the following year, Southern Company decided to spin off its remaining interest in Mirant. It is possible that Southern Company's own effort to undermine competition had made it less likely that Mirant could succeed, a point that was not disclosed to Mirant shareholders.

Mirant was doomed. Not only was competition a less profitable and more risky business than had at first been thought, but Mirant, like Enron, was deeply involved in the California fiasco. In little more than two years after it had been spun off, Mirant filed for bankruptcy. As the story unfolded, it became clear that Mirant, while still under Southern Company control, had purchased generators at greatly inflated prices. The purchases had probably been motivated by a desire to make a big splash and to gain market share and by a belief that competition would open more markets.

Southern Company had at first looked like a skyrocketing company, thanks to Mirant. As the *Atlanta Journal-Constitution* reported, its revenues climbed from $2.2 billion in 1999 to $31 billion in 2001 as a result of putting California's high energy prices on its books.[50] That made Southern Company number 52 in the Fortune 500. When realism crept in, Southern Company revenues fell to $8.5 billion in 2002, together with a Fortune 500 ranking of 259.

Mirant, now independent, claimed Southern Company knew that, despite its impressive numbers, its subsidiary was insolvent. It brought legal actions against its former parent seeking damages for harm to its shareholders. The Southern Company's foray into the competitive business had turned out to be a disaster but quite possibly one that it managed to dump on the unsuspecting investors who had bought into Mirant's apparently stunning success.

Southern Company was not finished with the competitive business —just a great deal more modest about it. Like many utilities, it had always sold excess power to neighboring utilities. This business had long predated EPAct and in fact it was the precursor of the Mirant gambit. It continued, giving the company considerable influence in the South.

While Southern Company's retail companies prefer to live under traditional regulation, Southern Power, a subsidiary, and the same retail companies get the benefit of industry restructuring by being allowed to sell power to third parties at market-based prices. FERC authorizes these prices, which may have little to do with the actual cost of service but allow the seller to price its power in line with supply and demand, provided the selling utility permits, at least in theory, others to sell to it under similar circumstances. The FERC policy requires that an entity enjoying the ability to set prices according to the market should not keep its own market under its absolute domination. If there is true competition, FERC expects that market rates will be lower than regulated rates.

While enjoying sales to others at market-based rates, Southern Company has engaged in a lengthy battle, still unresolved, with FERC over whether it has market domination where its subsidiaries sell at retail. It wants to retain the right to apply higher, state-regulated retail rates to its captive customers while being able to adjust prices—often lowering them—to meet competition in other markets. It admits that if FERC prevails, it will have to offer lower, market-based rates to its retail customers.

What Southern Company seeks is hardly unique among utilities. The largest players in the restructured world have acted similarly. While keeping industry restructuring at bay and maintaining traditional utility regulation in a monopoly market, they want to be able to take advantage of the new rules of competition in other markets. The rule they seek appears to be "what's mine is mine and what's yours is mine." Yet this outcome stands in direct opposition to the intent of EPAct and the regulatory deal that underpinned it: if you want free access to sell to others and need open-access transmission to do so, you, too, must be open to competition. In short, good intentions are not sufficient, and political and economic power have produced a distorted result.

Out of the hopes for an industry populated by many players including new nonutility entities has come an industry with fewer participants, and very few of them unaffiliated with the familiar utilities. Restructuring of the electric industry looks remarkably like the fruits of deregulation in other sectors: fewer, larger entities emerge. Regulation has become increasingly accommodating to large companies that can exercise considerable influence on how the market operates and on the rules that govern it. The traditional industry has found the way to persevere and grow. At the same time, the promise of an active, competitive market producing lower rates for the consumer has almost disappeared.

CHAPTER 8

LEGISLATORS AND REGULATORS

N o investor-owned utility cares about customers. It is not supposed to. Its purpose is to produce a return on the investment
of its shareholders and debt service for its bondholders. This simple
fact escapes most people who, if they even think about it, believe that
as "public" utilities, the companies must be imbued with some legal
obligation to their customers.

The investor-owned company has the same obligation to its customers as does any profit-making business: it wants to keep its customers happy so that they buy more of the product. When any
company faces competition, it is likely to try to please its customers
so that it can retain them. Because of the historical monopoly character of the utility business, state and local regulators were created
to provide the same effects as if there were competition. They are
supposed to require utility practice and, most important, utility

prices to meet the kind of pressures that would result from a competitive market. In other words, regulators make utilities care about customers.

The results have been far removed from this idealistic goal. The industry had been able to dominate the regulators. But if customers believe that utility regulation is supposed to protect them, they are wrong. The intent of utility regulation is to produce results in the "public" interest, not in the consumer interest. The quest for the public interest requires regulators to strike an undefined balance between what shareholders want as a return on their investment and what customers want in the form of fair prices and reliable service.

For example, in 2005, Westar Energy, a Kansas investor-owned utility, asked state regulators for a rate increase. The Citizens' Utility Ratepayer Board, representing small customers, proposed instead that rates be reduced. The utility argued the proposed decreases "would force the company into a struggle for survival."[51] The company had been placed in this position because of financial problems resulting from bad management, including the looting of the company by its former CEO. "To use past failures of others as a justification to debase current successes of incumbents would be arbitrary, even punitive," the new CEO stated. In other words, the rates that customers paid may have been too high when the company was being mismanaged and plundered, but because those events occurred in the past, the customers should never be compensated. Under this system, consumers would never get the chance to be protected, but the utility would be immune.

Legislatures Regulate

It all starts with legislatures, because regulation is a legislative function. Legislative bodies might opt to carry out detailed control of utilities but choose instead to delegate to independent bodies operating within legislative guidelines. Lawmakers avoid getting into regulation most of the time, because it is too complicated and too politically volatile. Much of the business of regulation consists of setting rates, and most of the time the rates are increasing. For obvious political reasons, no legislators want to be held responsible for higher electric bills, so they seek to avoid direct responsibility for utility rate increases, keeping their indirect role obscure.

Utility regulation is complicated, often involving sophisticated economic analysis. Lawmakers have neither the knowledge nor the time to delve into the details. They prefer instead to prescribe results, often suggested by the regulators themselves, and let the regulators figure out how to achieve them.

Because they are dependent on the favorable sentiment of the voters, legislators might be expected to set objectives that favor customers' interests, especially in seeking to lower the price of power. But legislators are also dependent on political contributions to their election campaigns. In many states, public utilities and their officers are among the largest contributors to political campaigns. In the three federal elections between 2000 and 2004, electric utilities and their employees contributed $56.3 million, of which 63 percent went to Republicans.[52] In 2002 alone, the Southern Company led the group with $1.923 million, 68 percent of which went to the GOP. Exelon was in second place and similarly favored the Republicans. The utilities also deploy corps of lobbyists to influence legislators during their legislative sessions. Customers, unless they are large industrials, usually have no such representation in the legislative process—they have little influence, contribute relatively little political money, and have only a handful of volunteer lobbyists.

Until the energy crisis in 1973, nearly all state legislatures were lulled into complacency by the belief that electricity prices were low and did not need their attention. As a small part of the household or corporate budget, the cost of electricity did not rise to visibility as a major political issue. Legislatures did not concern themselves with the possibility that monopolies were dispensable or that utilities might be making more profit than they merited. Politically, lawmakers could tell themselves that they were looking out for people who depended on utility dividends, which were steady if unspectacular.

A good crisis gets the attention of government; legislators want to avoid the stigma of failing to cope with an emergency. The sharp increase in energy prices after 1973 required government action, and state legislatures felt that the scope of the problem required federal action, but the crisis lingered while Washington dithered. The state response was to allow utilities to pass their increased fuel costs directly through to their customers, protecting the companies from any loss of profit and from any real responsibility for shifting to lower-cost fuels. This policy was based on the belief that if customers felt the full impact of the increased cost of fuel, they would be forced to conserve. Conservation by price was probably the most effective policy, but it absolved everybody except the consumers from responsibility. To be sure, conservation could cause utilities to lose revenues needed to cover the costs of their fixed operations, such as wires and customer billing, but they could and would seek rate increases to cover the loss. In the only gesture toward making the utilities face the new reality, legislatures banned them from using customer revenues for advertising to promote the use of electricity.

When Congress finally acted to create PURPA in 1978, state reactions were varied, with some actively applying the law and others trying to ignore it; the results across the country were negligible. In fact, in many places the principal result was higher rates for customers. As with responses to many other crises, the government solution was to throw money at the problem, and this time the dollars came from electricity customers.

Under Presidents Reagan and George H. W. Bush, economic conservatism became the standard for setting regulatory policy. After the passage of EPAct in 1992, just as with PURPA, states had the option of whether or not to fall into line with federal utility policy. The decision whether or not to open state retail markets to competition was left to state legislatures. Much as with PURPA, some enthusiastically supported the extension of competition, however untried it was, while others not only declined to consider it but even supported efforts to undermine wholesale competition. The lineup was remarkably similar for the two pieces of federal legislation: the Northeast and California, high-cost areas, supported both, and the South and West opposed both. The deciding factor was price. Where the price of electricity was high enough to attract voter interest, lawmakers could more easily resist utility pressure and were able to legislate change. Where the need for change seemed less apparent to legislators, the utilities continued to dominate.

Those state legislatures that wanted to restrict change so that it applied only to the wholesale business were reasonable. Little was known about how electric markets would work, but there was considerable experience with wholesale electric sales to municipal utilities, rural electric cooperatives, and other utilities. Though most previous wholesale transactions had not taken place in a truly open market setting, wholesale markets could be a reasonable start. Once the market for these sales developed, it would be possible to consider the extension of competition. This is probably what Congress had in mind.

However, few states, if any, actually articulated this or any theoretical underpinning for their policies other than the simple desire to see lower prices. The best that could be said for some states, from Washington State to Georgia, was that they wanted to protect their own regulatory turf and resented federal intrusion into what had traditionally been state jurisdiction. They chose not to introduce retail access because of their attachment to gradualism or the status quo. They resisted federal market rules because of the stated belief that there need be no uniform national approach and the publicly unstated belief that FERC did not know what it was doing. Many states that declined to adopt retail access, such as those stretching along the East Coast from North Carolina to Louisiana, accepted all these arguments but went further. They were reluctant to support opening the transmission grid to competition even at the wholesale level and backed utilities in their efforts to keep transmission from falling under independent management.

Where states enthusiastically adopted open access, the legislatures seemed to accept blindly that the market was a safe and adequate replacement for regulation. They believed that they had learned much over decades about how commodity markets operated and that what they had learned could be applied to electricity. And they were firmly but erroneously convinced that electric service was like telephone service and that active competition would produce lower rates. Not only were there virtually no new state rules for regulating the market, but most of the normal consumer protection guidelines were omitted. The lack of explicit consumer protection resulted in part because the legislatures believed that utility regulators would simply act to meet the need for controls, if any, or that there would be such vigorous competition that the market itself would soon wash out the dishonest.

An important semantic distinction tells the story. Legislators and others talked about what was happening in the electric industry as "deregulation." They believed that government prescribed too many controls for the electric industry, which now deserved to be deregulated. Generators, traditionally subject to regulation of their costs and the assured recovery of them from customers, were now deregulated and left to the mercy of the market, relieving the customer of some risk. Legislators wanted the invisible hand of the market to replace the heavy hand of regulation. However, it was only generators and not the industry itself that had been deregulated.

However, the correct term to describe what was happening was industry "restructuring," not deregulation. Turning the transmission lines into common carriers for wholesale, retail, or both would give the industry a new structure. By deregulating generation, EPAct and the state rules and laws mandated at least the partial unbundling of the traditional utility. To be sure, those states that ignored the intent of the law and blocked unbundling or carried it out more in form than in substance did not even deregulate generation, in deference to the utilities.

"Restructuring" was not the same thing as "deregulation," but legislatures appeared to miss the distinction. They failed to see the need to replace the comprehensive regulatory regime applying to the bundled utility with measures that would replace the inherent safeguards of the old system with consumer protection suitable to the new system. As Enron showed, the new players could easily manipulate the market. Even worse, they might not be able to keep their commitments to customers to provide service, a failing that never occurred with the bundled utility.

In their enthusiasm for "deregulation," most state legislatures that introduced retail access violated the cardinal rules of competition, namely, that the open market should set the price. Eager to show the benefits of the market to their constituents and perhaps fearful that the power companies might seize those benefits for themselves, legislatures in California, Ohio, and other states mandated caps on retail prices. The legislators could return to their districts and proclaim that they had deregulated electricity and that prices would be cut immediately by, say, 10 percent. They did not need to explain that the price cut did not result from the operation of the market but from legislative fiat. In fact, they probably failed to understand that by setting the low rates to be charged by the incumbent utility, presumably still having access to its own generators, they had discouraged new market entrants, who were supposed to be encouraged by the creation of an open market. The new players simply could not beat the legislatively mandated price.

Take, for example, a decision by WPS Energy Services, a marketer, to withdraw from parts of the Ohio market and no longer serve FirstEnergy customers in Cleveland and Euclid after the end of 2005. FirstEnergy had initiated a Rate Stabilization Plan (RSP), including a special surcharge to apply to the default standard offer service in effect until the end of 2008. A customer could avoid paying the surcharge only by giving FirstEnergy one year's notice of its intent to switch to a competitive supplier. Such a switch would be unlikely, because the RSP price was below the market price available from others. If FirstEnergy could not recover its true costs because of this low price, it could defer the shortfall so that it could be collected with interest from customers well after 2008. WPS Energy had no way to borrow money to defer some of its own costs as it had no regulatory guarantee that the cost of debt service could be recovered later. It had to withdraw. Although what caused the withdrawal was a regulatory decision, it could only have been made possible by state laws that mandated "rate stability," despite Ohio's pride in having an open market. The legislature had both created and undermined the market.

The Surcharge Habit

State legislatures have actually become players themselves and raised the cost of electricity. In the belief that the market will produce lower prices or because such prices have been mandated, lawmakers see no harm in tacking a variety of surcharges onto electric bills. In effect, legislatures find it possible to impose taxation through utility bills in the belief that nobody will notice because the market will bring prices down.

The most egregious of these surcharges is the low-income or universal service charge. If people have difficulty paying their electric bill, other customers must pay the cost of subsidizing them. This hidden tax is actually a reflection of social policy and has little to do with utility rates. Low-income heating oil customers also receive assistance, but the funds are derived from public tax revenues, not a surcharge on those using oil. The social policy for electricity similarly reflects the electorate's values; the method of financing reflects the method legislatures use to achieve the policy without seeming to incur any cost. A kind of legislative greed encourages them to avoid a policy under which all help those less able to pay, instead taxing only electricity customers. If the state can raise funds for a social policy without explicitly raising broad-based taxes, legislators get the credit but not the responsibility. In Maine, when the state received a large windfall tax payment, and the governor's representatives and other parties came up with the idea to use it for a permanent fund that would support low-income aid, the legislature rejected the proposal and gobbled up the money for current spending. The surcharge on electric bills survived.

Legislatures frequently use another surcharge to collect revenues to promote conservation. At the same time as the distribution companies are promoting the use of electricity to increase their revenues, the states try to encourage reduced consumption through official conservation programs funded by customers. More money is collected for these programs if the customers use more electricity. The absurdity of this policy seems to escape legislators.

Where retail access exists, many states require that customers pay off the utility investment that can no longer be recovered directly. Costs relating to investment in failed power plants or in high-cost PURPA contracts that have been bought off are called "regulatory assets," and the customers are forced to pay the utilities to cover these costs. The power companies are relieved of responsibility for their bad investment decisions, and customers keep paying for generators for many years though they get no power from them. Government is relieved of its responsibility for unwise PURPA decisions, as contracts are paid off at unreasonable prices. These charges recover "stranded costs," but the costs are actually only temporarily marooned, not actually stranded. The customers will rescue them.

Eventually stranded costs are paid off. Rates may go down, but utilities may seek to hold onto the revenues or legislatures may come up with new surcharges. In Ohio, there are eight different surcharges that may be tacked onto bills. There and elsewhere, surcharges show no signs of disappearing. Using the utility as tax collector is an idea that is here to stay.

At the federal legislative level, Congress intervenes in the electric business less often but with great effect. Milestone laws—the Federal Power Act, PUHCA, PURPA, and EPAct—spread over seventy years demonstrated both a legislative recognition of issues that needed to be addressed and a desire to allow a regulatory body, first the Federal Power Commission, then the SEC, and finally FERC, to deal with these issues. The regulators have been given broad authority subject to review more by the federal courts than by

Congress itself. In the absence of crises, the legislative branch has been content to keep its distance from utility business.

The 1992 EPAct and the Electricity Modernization Act of 2005, which formed part of the major 2005 energy law (called EPAct 2005), represented the first major shift in regulatory policy since the Kennedy administration fostered more serious scrutiny of the wholesale business and transmission, as we shall see. The new laws, both passed under a Bush presidency, were aimed at moving away from comprehensive regulation toward a market system where competition would control more than bureaucrats would. The 2005 law also added tax incentives to support the power companies and to encourage more efficient energy use.

Like many other bills passed by Congress, the 2005 law was a Christmas tree with goodies for many. With this law, the legislative branch chose to enter into the details of regulatory issues. For the first time, the law recognized "native load," the customers to whom a distribution company is obligated to provide service. In effect, this was a victory for the still-bundled utilities by helping them in their attempt to have a priority right to use the transmission lines they own to serve their own customers. Also for the first time, it brought consumer-owned utilities and federal power marketing authorities under the same obligations to provide transmission access as had been imposed on investor-owned utilities. The biggest gift that Congress offered the utilities was the repeal of PUHCA.

In its place, Congress authorized FERC to have access to holding company records as "necessary or appropriate for the protection of utility customers with respect to jurisdictional rates [those under FERC's control]." State regulators were assured of similar access. The guarantee of access was a positive move, but the condition that it can be obtained only with respect to rates and not other potential utility abuses may prove to undermine the value of the compensation paid for the repeal of PUHCA. FERC was also given the authority formerly given to the SEC to review holding company mergers and acquisitions.

Not only did the law repeal PUHCA, it also eviscerated PURPA. The requirement placed on utilities to purchase from qualifying facilities ended. Utilities are now allowed to become PURPA power producers. Although the law had fallen into disuse because the use of avoided cost had become far less aggressive, the PURPA changes effectively ended the bold initiative that had led to industry restructuring. The utilities had won.

The 2005 law also dealt with two embarrassing problems for the industry: the Enron crisis and the blackout of 2003. FERC had blamed its failure to respond promptly to the market situation in California on its apparent lack of authority to provide the necessary remedies. The new law allowed FERC to adopt rules to obtain timely information, prohibited the filing of false information, and banned "any manipulative or deceptive device or contrivance" in the electric energy market or in purchasing and selling transmission services. The horse is gone, and the barn door is now firmly locked. Enron set back the operation of the competitive market so far that this language, laudable but late, is likely to do little to restore confidence. And in the new law, as we have seen, Washington finally took the first steps to prevent a recurrence of the blackout of 2003.

The 2005 energy law expanded on a theme in federal electricity regulation that began to emerge at the time of PURPA. Although state regulation predates federal authority and is more extensive in many ways, the states are increasingly coming under federal control. Federal law now tells state regulators how to conduct their business without any need for state legislatures, normally required to authorize any state regulatory authority, to get involved. State regulatory commissions are required under the 2005 law to decide if utilities must adopt any conservation measures, though the law does not prejudge the decisions the state commissions may make.

Regulators in an Unknown World

While federal and state legislative interest in electric industry matters is sporadic, the regulators are always present. For much of the industry's history, state regulation was weak and mostly accommodated the utilities. Because electricity was first seen as a luxury item, there was no pressing need to protect consumers. As its use spread, the revolution that it brought led consumers and regulators to ignore abuses by the electric utilities. Uncontested rate increases were common, and nobody intervened on behalf of customers. It was not unusual for utilities to draft the orders approving their own actions for state commissions to issue.

The 1973 energy crisis brought a noticeable increase in state regulation. Higher costs meant higher rates and greater interest in the regulators' decisions. Utilities found themselves facing vocal critics more often than anytime in the past. Still, forced to deal with higher fuel supply prices, utilities and regulators agreed on the automatic pass-through of these new costs. Fuel-cost adjustments became the standard of the utility industry, while airlines and others dependent on fuel were struggling to keep costs under control and limit pass-throughs. Some regulators began to look for ways to promote the more efficient use of electricity and later to apply PURPA.

State regulators have never had the same degree of knowledge about utility operations as the utilities themselves. While utilities employ scores of engineers, few state bodies have more than one or two electrical engineers. The regulated utility simply asserts that costs are necessary to keep the company functioning, and the regulators have no way to dispute those costs or to know whether the utility is operating efficiently or even safely. Consumers could easily have a false sense of security that state regulators were closely watching the companies. As for the costs passed on to customers, most are accepted without question. This has always been the essential flaw in state utility regulation. In dealing with bundled utilities under the traditional format—still the practice in most states—regulators approve a revenue requirement sufficient to cover the "cost of service." Nearly all of the data to prove that costs have been incurred and that such costs are reasonable come from the utilities themselves. Regulatory staffs may single out a few items for close scrutiny, which usually means asking the utility for even more data, but they accept without question most of the data filed. If the cost of a specific activity has previously been approved, the regulators usually look only at the changes proposed and do not question the underlying cost. Even more curious is the fact that the utility is not required to spend the funds it receives on the purposes for which it has been allowed to recover them from customers. To be sure, if it cannot show that it spent the money on specific functions, the cost basis for those functions will decline in future rate cases. But who determines that the data presented by the utilities accurately reflect the way the money was spent? If there are no visible problems caused by the utility's operations, then no regulator audits their books, though outside audits are required. However, independent outside audits do not get into the detail of operations.

Occasionally, a utility faces extraordinary costs. These costs may be imposed by nature or man. Hurricane Kristina added unexpected spending to the budget of Entergy, a major utility operating in Louisiana. The solution to the California crisis—expensive long-term contracts—added new costs to the operating utilities. Regulators usually allow those costs to be recovered by a surcharge built into rates, which spreads the recovery over several years. In California, the costs were financed by debt, which will be repaid over a long period. The utility is allowed to recover the full amount of the additional costs from its customers. In other words, customers bear the entire risk, not shareholders.

In responding to Katrina, Entergy's Louisiana subsidiary went even further. It lobbied federal and state officials not only for the recovery of its hurricane-related costs but also for lost revenue. People did not pay for electricity when the lines were down, leaving Entergy with some uncompensated expenses and lost profits. While the owner of a local grocery store might get insurance payments for damages, he or she would have lost sales and the related revenues; no government could compel the store's customers to make up for the lost sales. But Entergy expected to be made whole by its customers. Its Louisiana subsidiary also considered filing for bankruptcy.

The only consideration of costs in which the regulator's financial staff expertise might match that of the utilities was in setting the allowed profit. Although much analysis of appropriate margins takes place, the state regulatory commission has considerable discretionary authority and can reward or punish utilities by their profit allowances, known as return on equity. Parties opposing rate increases put before the commission their own views on the proper level of return. Once the commission makes a decision, the allowed return remains in place until the next rate review, a period that may continue while returns in the unregulated market fluctuate. In fact, most levels of return granted by state commissions—9 to 14 percent —are at or above what an investor could expect in the normal financial markets. Performance-based rates allow utilities to earn an even greater profit. Few investors could expect the level of returns routinely allowed the utilities by regulators, especially for such safe investments.

State regulation might offer customers some degree of protection,

especially if they found knowledgeable representatives to participate in the process, but even after state regulators became more
aggressive in the 1970s, utility interests continued to dominate. In
some states, competent staff struggled to keep up with the utilities,
and occasionally did. Mostly, regulation in these states was vigorous but not greatly effective. In other states, the utilities continued to dominate the legislative and regulatory scene.

In most states, members of regulatory commissions are appointed
by the governor, usually subject to legislative confirmation. Frequently, commission membership turns over with the election of a
new governor, suggesting that the posts are something of a political
plum. This effect is somewhat attenuated by staggered terms in
some states, which can make it difficult for a governor to change the
complexion of state regulation immediately after election. In Virginia and South Carolina, the legislature rather than the governor
gets to dole out the positions.

In eleven states, commission members are chosen by direct popular vote. These states are all in the South and West. Four—Montana, North Dakota, South Dakota, and Nebraska—began electing
commissioners when populism was at its peak. The principal states
served by the Southern Company and Entergy—Georgia, Alabama,
Mississippi, and Louisiana—have elected commissions. Arizona,
New Mexico, and Oklahoma, striving to insure complete regulatory
independence, provide for their commissions and the election of
commissioners in the state constitution, in contrast with most
states, which create regulatory bodies by law.

While in theory direct popular election should mean that commissions are more responsive to consumers, the cost of political
campaigns undermines that hypothesis. Running for a state commission is much like any other political campaign, and candidates
with access to support from the utilities are likely to be well

funded. The utilities in such states may also have significant influence on the legislatures. Of the eleven states with elected commissions, only one has pursued retail access, and then only to a limited
extent. Three others initiated the process but suspended it. Three in
the upper Midwest rely on public power for a significant part of
their supply. Four in the South reflect the preferences of the dominant investor-owned utilities.

Direct election of state regulatory commissions has not produced
results in terms of either consumer protection or industry restructuring that differ from the outcomes in the other states. Election is
either consistent with a state tradition favoring consumer-owned
power or reflects an effective method for utilities to dominate the
regulatory process. Many elected commissioners display independence, but few demonstrate any particular merit in the elective over
the appointive process. At best, election to a state commission can
be a stepping-stone to higher elective office or simply the reward at
the end of an elective career.

Who are state commissioners? In states that elect them, they are
often politicians. In Arizona in 2005, four were former legislators,
and one was a former newspaper reporter who wrote a graduate
thesis on electric deregulation. Georgia's five elected commissioners
included a former legislator, a medical administrator, a lawyer, an
elected county commissioner, and a former commission staff
member who obtained office through appointment to fill a vacancy.

Appointed commissioners are likely to be better qualified. The
Illinois commission's members have included a former staff member,
an administrative law judge, a former state government official, a
teacher, and a corporate officer. In 2005, the New York Commission
was composed of a former energy agency official, a judge, a New York
City regulator, a manufacturer, and a former legislator. The three-
member Kansas commission included that year two regulators and

an energy industry executive. Appointed commissions often reflect political balance by including women and minorities. They are less likely to reflect political affiliation, which may not even be disclosed. Elected commissions are often chosen in partisan contests.

According to the Center for Public Integrity, a public policy watchdog, 42 percent of state commissioners come to their job as former legislators or other political officials. About 13 percent come from the industries they regulate. Financial disclosure by commissioners of any investments in those industries is poor or nonexistent in a majority of states. Where there is disclosure, about one fifth of the commissioners reveal that they or their spouses have such investments and some accept speaking engagement fees from regulated entities. Yet when Martin Cohen, the former director of the Illinois Citizen's Utility Board, was nominated chairman of the Illinois Commerce Commission, he failed to be confirmed. One senator complained that Cohen "has a certain bias against utility companies."[53]

For regulatory qualifications, few can top Joseph Swidler, appointed general counsel of the TVA, President Kennedy's chairman of the Federal Power Commission, and later chairman of the New York Commission. He is rivaled by Peter Bradford, who was appointed as chairman of the Maine Commission, then as member of the Nuclear Regulatory Commission, returned to the Maine chairmanship after a brief stint as Maine public advocate, and finally headed up the New York Commission. Neither Swidler nor Bradford was regarded as a friend of the industry. These were all appointed positions, and Swidler's commission appointments came from both a Democrat and a Republican.

State commissions cannot be relied upon to produce results that benefit customers. Their obligation to the public interest, balancing the needs of customers and utilities, often results in customers bearing the burden of proving the utilities wrong. Because of their political dominance and their control of most of the data on which regulatory decisions are based, utilities set their own terms for the debate. Regulators are exposed more persistently to utility advocates than to those representing customers, and this socialization takes its toll. Regulators lack the tools and the expertise to judge many complex issues. State utility regulation, though not corrupt, is frequently inept and opinionated and often not effective. When distinguished regulators emerge, their impact is notable because of their relative rarity.

Federal regulation of the electric industry began later and progressed more slowly than state regulation. The evolution of federal action depended on the FPC gaining a clear understanding of what constituted interstate commerce. Gradually, as it became accepted that electrons pass over the lines without regard to political boundaries, the FPC assumed jurisdiction over high-voltage transmission lines and wholesale sales. But these developments would not have any significant effect until the 1960s. Meanwhile, the FPC's principal focus was on natural gas, with only a small amount of staff time devoted to electricity.

In the wake of the 1973 energy crisis, President Carter's energy policy included a start toward giving FERC, the successor of the FPC, increased regulatory clout. But FERC could only be as good as its members and staff. Appointments to the commission continued to be highly political, with each president seeking to obtain support for his policy goals partly through the people he placed on the panel instead of developing a group of competent and professional regulators with tenures more akin to the lengthy terms of judges than to those of cabinet officers. FERC commissioners come and go with changes in the White House occupant or even mere shifts in policy. It is quite likely that within any five-year interval, the entire membership of the commission will have changed.

Competent people often serve as commissioners, but the commission is never more than a stepping-stone along their career path. Recent chairs illustrate the point. Martin Allday, a Texas oil and gas lawyer and friend of G. H. W. Bush, resumed his career. Martha Hesse joined utility boards of directors. Betsy Moler became a senior officer of Exelon, the huge Chicago-based electric utility. James Hoecker developed his utility practice in a large Washington, D.C., law firm. Curt Hébert went to a top position at Entergy, another of the leading utilities.

The FERC staff, which includes many highly competent professionals, suffers from the same problems as most state commission staffs. It does not have members who are as technically familiar with many relevant matters that come before FERC as the industry representatives are. Historically, the technical staff has been forced to take on trust much that a larger and better-trained group would have examined. In fact, FERC has said that it does not actually regulate utility operations. Even before the 2005 law, that meant that nobody seemed to regulate transmission. In addition, FERC is supposed to audit financial data that utilities rely upon in their rate filings, but it does so only sporadically and with great delays.

Coupled with this historical weakness is FERC's obvious unfamiliarity with market regulation. Almost from the outset of developing rules for EPAct, the commission saw its role as not only to set the rules for open-access transmission but also to prescribe the rules for the operation of power markets. In effect, it cut back its role as a regulator of the actions of others and began to prescribe how they must act. In laying out market rules, the commission relied heavily on appealing but untested theoretical constructs developed by its staff and others.

The staff itself was populated by people with no practical market experience. They assumed that the creation of competition would benefit customers and that more competition would bring more benefit. For example, they thought that short-term sales were better than long-term sales because they sent more accurate price signals. This single judgment, which continues to have a broad effect, placed the hoped-for price effect ahead of the stability and certainty valued by many customers in purchasing electricity.

In their enthusiasm upon entering the new world of competition, both commissioners and staff wanted to act as quickly as possible. New mandates and policies came forth at an unprecedented pace. The rate of change alarmed many major players and confused others. Compliance required huge expenditures, which would have to be recovered from customers.

As FERC regulators faced the opportunities resulting from the passage of EPAct, they were not prepared either to deal with the key players—as would soon be illustrated by Enron—nor to respond to the needs of customers. In effect, customers would be sacrificed on the altar of theory, led by high priests who had little awareness of the practical results and dangers that could arise from putting their theories into practice.

Even before passage of the 1992 EPAct, wholesale customers began to probe the opportunities for more effective use of the transmission system to acquire alternative power supply. Because there was as yet no open access, the FPC and then FERC had to decide the rates for use of transmission service if utilities were willing to provide it. Although FERC could not force utilities to transmit or "wheel" power to wholesale customers, it could make approval of other requests by the utilities conditional on their willingness to provide third-party transmission. And wholesale customers were more likely to get a fair price determination for power supply from federal regulators than they could get from their state authorities.

Even if states had good intentions, federal regulation prevailed.

For example, when Rhode Island, long before restructuring, tried to force shareholders to absorb some costs rather than making customers pay what it deemed to be an excessive wholesale rate, the state was denied the right to do so by the U.S. Supreme Court, which upheld the federal regulator because of the supremacy of federal law over state law.[54]

FERC Makes the Market

EPAct moved electricity from the margins of FERC interest to the center of attention. Because the law now required transmission owners to wheel power for anybody from generators to marketers to wholesale customers, FERC needed to devise rules to insure that the law was applied. At first, transactions began to take place much as they had in the past on a voluntary basis, but FERC wanted to promote even more access.

One problem in undertaking power purchase transactions, even under the new law, was that each power purchaser had to pay for transmission service from each utility whose system was used to bring power to it. If a deal crossed more than one system, it was said that rates "pancaked," or piled one on top of another. FERC decided to promote the merger of transmission systems, at least operationally, so that they could charge a single rate for transactions going across more than one company's grid. The results could be startling. Some transactions in the small, six-state New England region stood to pay only one charge instead of as many as four. The states in the Northeast that had already been working together to insure system reliability, stretching from the District of Columbia to Maine, were the most responsive to bringing their transmission systems under common control. The application of a single rate provided lower costs to wholesale customers, including investor-owned utilities buying and selling to one another. Of course, congestion on the transmission lines, creating physical barriers to flows of power, could undercut the value of this reform.

At first the commission focused on creating rules for transmission access that would be uniform across the country and that promoted—but did not require—that interconnected systems create larger transmission groups. It delegated some of its regulatory authority to regional groups, provided they could not be dominated by the transmission owners. It ordered the posting of information on a public Internet Web site—called an Open Access Same-Time Information System (OASIS), so that potential users could learn how much transmission space was available. The commission also said that it would order new transmission to be built when needed to meet demand, subject to state siting approval. It also determined that it had the right to order utilities to establish a transmission rate that would apply not only to marketers seeking to make wholesale sales but to the utilities themselves in serving their native load. The major utilities bristled at this change but prepared to comply, though later they would successfully undermine FERC's intent. Taken together, these sweeping measures were an aggressive and positive package to make the grid available for the use of competitors. But this was not deregulation; FERC insisted that it would continue to control transmission and wholesale sales.

FERC was pressed to go further and faster. If the grid were now open to all, FERC concluded, there should be a market for electric power that took better advantage of open access than simply making easier one-on-one deals on the traditional wholesale model. The market could also allow for daily transactions to take place, which would let customers experience the current price of power, just as they did for other products, rather than an artificial price.

The traditional utility giants stood by nervously to see if their dominance would be threatened by the coming changes.

The regulators also changed. The new president, George W. Bush, appointed Pat Wood, the former head of the Texas commission, to be FERC chairman. With Texas touting its successful launch of competition, Wood was in the limelight. He was strongly favored by Enron as a regulator sympathetic to marketers.

As proposals for the market were developed, regulation became a highly complex system designed to duplicate as closely as possible the traditional commodity markets that had grown up over decades. However, all of the major rules that FERC adopted would promote a marketplace dominated by a few large players and would override consumer preferences. The new system was intended to replace the usual fixed-price, long-term deals with more price-sensitive deals. Regulators did not care about customer preference for long-term arrangements that provided stability. Nor were they concerned that the highly complex system they were creating drove potential competitors out of the market. Only large, interstate players had sufficient resources to participate in the market.

The crowning element of the FERC market initiatives was SMD (the Standard Market Design requiring that all power markets in the United States would operate under a single set of rules), which failed. With its attention on creating a market, even before SMD, FERC went lightly when it came to safeguards. Neither the commissioners nor the staff had expertise in dealing with markets. The commission had apparently come to believe that the potential power of its regulatory authority would continue to bring market participants into compliance with the letter and spirit of the rules, just as with its traditional role. Some FERC people wondered if the commission had the authority to deal with market manipulation.

When the California crisis broke, the initial FERC reaction to the state government's charges of market manipulation was disbelief bordering on scorn. The commission preferred to see the situation as the fault of state incompetence and lack of adequate transmission and generation resources because the state had placed too much emphasis on environmental protection and too little on power supply. As evidence mounted that state officials had correctly diagnosed the problem, FERC seemed to look for ways to conclude that it had little legal authority to deal with the situation. It made a futile and bizarre attempt to dump the board of directors of the California ISO.

Eventually, the commission was forced to take a more critical look at the California situation. It had begun to appear that FERC was favoring Enron, the president's friend, and ignoring the Democratic governor of California. The commission slowly began to respond to the critical situation by offering the opportunity for some refunds, but its action came too late to save FERC from the political embarrassment of its failure to take the situation seriously. The Enron scandal soured the willingness of players to take risks in the electricity market and undermined the market. While the new energy bill would give FERC more explicit authority to deal with crises like the one it had mishandled in California, it was legitimate to ask if the commission could have used its existing powers more effectively.

While the commission might have been able to force SMD on reluctant utilities when it was riding the crest of the Bush administration's success, it no longer had any chance of doing so when the California crisis revealed its own weakness. Enron had lost its clout at the White House as the prime representative of the marketers. The Southern Company and its allies were no longer wary of the Texas power marketer's ability to call the shots at FERC. States and utilities in the South and West stiffened their resistance to SMD, and it was gone.

So was Pat Wood. The White House understood that some of its major supporters did not like Wood's policies, and Enron was a liability where once it had been a valuable ally. Learning of rumors that the major utilities might try to embarrass Wood at a Senate confirmation hearing for a new term, the White House decided to go with another candidate.

More than a dozen years after the passage of EPAct, FERC had created a sound set of rules for open transmission access, but its attention had been diverted from perfecting the application of those rules and insuring that wholesale competition could grow and benefit from these legislatively mandated changes. It had become preoccupied with markets, about which it knew relatively little, especially concerning market abuse. The results were a disjointed and often malfunctioning system costing more to manage than ever before and resulting in the dominance of the industry by a handful of giant corporations.

As for the other branches of government, both the executive and judicial branch play limited roles. The legislative branch has the leading role, leaving regulators to deal with the application in detail of broad legislative principles. Presidents and governors have long realized that regulation can often result in higher rates and that it is prudent to allow independent and often anonymous regulators to make the hard decisions.

The courts will not second-guess judgments by regulators, who are supposedly experts on the matters they regulate. Instead, courts usually limit their decisions to determining if the regulatory body's judgments are within legal limits. The result is both considerable regulatory independence and a great deal of unchecked power. A decision by a federal or state regulator, whose very existence is obscure if not invisible to many, is usually the first and last time a matter is reviewed.

Legislators and regulators offer consumers only limited protection against the excesses of utilities: rates too high or actions too greedy. Recent history suggests that those who should have protected customers lost their way when dealing with the electric industry.

CHAPTER 9

THE SURVIVOR AND OTHER FRIENDS OF THE CONSUMER

T hroughout the history of the electric industry, consumer interests have been either ignored or misunderstood. The challenge
for both utilities and regulators has been to manage the industry
just below the level of consumer discontent, with reliability high
enough and prices low enough to avoid consumer outcry.

Utilities, which want to keep customers captive, regulators, who
commit customers to high costs in the pursuit of elusive long-term
benefits, and legislatures, which see customers as sources of revenue for public purposes, all fail to listen to what the consumers
want. Electric industry policy has always been arrogant if not
exploitive.

From the viewpoint of the industry, regulators, and government,
electricity customers are "ratepayers," the people who pay the bills.
The customers see themselves as "consumers."

Electricity Providers 2003		
Publicly owned Utilities	2,010	61.3%
Cooperatives	885	27.0%
Investor-owned Utilities	223	6.8%
Power Marketers	150	4.6%
Federal Power Agencies	9	0.3%
	3,277	

Source: American Public Power Association

The electric consumer has only a few friends: municipal electric utilities, rural cooperatives, and state consumer advocates.

EPAct was drafted to cover only wholesale transactions—power purchases by utilities and their suppliers. Any utility would qualify. The larger investor-owned utilities would benefit, though in most cases they would continue to produce most of their own power and purchase only a small portion of their requirements. But two classes of utilities, the municipals (commonly called "munis") and the rural cooperatives generally purchased most or even all of their power from others. Selling about 20 percent of the power in the United States, they stood to be the most obvious gainers from EPAct.

These utilities had often been the captive customers of the larger, investor-owned utilities to which they were connected. Some purchased what was called "all-requirements service," meaning that in effect the "host" utility would supply them with power in much the same way as it supplied its own customers. Many co-ops and most munis had little bargaining power and were obliged to accept what was offered. Under EPAct they would be free to shop for power supply, and the host utility would be obligated to transmit it at FERC-approved rates.

Under federal law, these consumer-owned utilities had preferential access to power generated at taxpayer-financed facilities. That meant that transmission owners had been transmitting power for them at FERC-approved rates. Some transmission owners had voluntarily offered transmission access to wholesale customers. In short, transmission access for the traditional wholesale customers was not new, but it could be easier and greatly expanded.

In 1993, well before FERC had written any rules to create power markets, consumer-owned utilities began to take advantage of the opportunities created by EPAct. In perhaps the first major transaction under the new law, Maine's Madison Electric Works (MEW) asked several New England utilities to make proposals to serve it. It had long been a customer of Central Maine Power (CMP), the largest electric utility in the state, and had even turned over its largest customer, Madison Paper Industries, directly to CMP to serve. It now proposed to begin serving the paper company and, if necessary, to force CMP to transmit power from another supplier. CMP refused to take seriously the possible loss of MEW and the paper company, representing three percent of its load, and would not bid. The competition was heated, and MEW finally selected Connecticut-based Northeast Utilities, the largest company in New England, as its new supplier. CMP sought but failed to stop the process by litigation. When the matter was finally resolved, MEW customers received a rate reduction of more than 40 percent and the president of CMP lost his job.

Public Power and Its Wars

Some of earliest electric companies were founded by local governments to insure that their constituents would have access to electricity. The first municipal utilities were founded in the 1880s. Maine's MEW dates from 1888, just six years after Edison opened the Pearl Street Station. At about the same time, small investor-owned utilities began to be created. Over the following decades, larger utilities arose, mainly through investor-owned companies purchasing others, including some owned by municipalities. Many municipal utilities survived this wave of acquisitions, and others continued to be created as new areas of the country became populated. Today they exist in forty-nine states. Of the 2,010 public power entities, the largest is in Los Angeles with 1.5 million customers, and there are sixty-eight with fewer than eleven customers.[55] As low-cost suppliers, they have long been engaged in fighting off efforts by the power companies to eliminate the advantages that benefit their customers.

Public power, a term that includes munis and other similar government-owned electric utilities, produces lower electric rates than investor-owned utilities. Almost entirely financed by debt, munis raise their funds in the tax-exempt municipal finance market. As parts of government itself, the municipal utilities do not pay taxes. They generally serve compact areas, making it less costly for them to connect with their customers than is the case for other utilities. While both co-ops and munis are usually exempt from most state utility regulation, co-ops are in effect regulated by their government-approved lenders. Munis are more independent. In all these respects, munis differ from co-ops.

Munis have long enjoyed a preferential right to power generated at dams built on the navigable waters of the United States. Lawyers joke that the definition of a navigable stream is any body of water in which "you can float a Supreme Court decision." The underlying notion guiding this policy is that these waters are public assets, fundamental to interstate commerce, whose value should go to the public. As early as 1906, federal law provided that municipal utilities, as public entities, would have a preference in buying power from federally financed electric generators. Under the 1920 Federal Water Power Act, Congress said that the preference should include all dams built on navigable waters.

This legislation predated the formation of the FPC and was intended primarily to deal with the accelerated development of hydroelectric production to support the increased productive capacity of the United States required by World War I. Although Congress clearly favored municipal (and later, co-op) preference, during the war it authorized investor-owned power companies to develop hydro power. This authorization, which gave power companies fifty-year licenses, was designed to bring dams into production rapidly. The Federal Water Power Act codified this policy.

The application of this law was to cause a lengthy battle between investor-owned and consumer-owned utilities that would do much to shape the character of the power industry. Investor-owned utilities, working through the Edison Electric Institute (EEI), their trade organization, were resolved to undermine preference power for fear that the municipals would gain access to a large share of the country's power production.

The power companies had always been unhappily aware of the price advantage that municipals gained from their preference in the use of power from federal dams, and their concern grew as large new public power entities were being created. In 1946, Republicans gained control of Congress, and the power companies believed they had the opportunity to strip municipals of their advantages. The GOP attempted to eliminate municipal preference by mandating that power from federal facilities would be sold at the generator itself to any purchaser, thus removing both preference power and the requirement to transmit to the purchaser. Another bill, also inspired by the drive to kill preference power, called for Savannah River Electric to be authorized to install its own generator at a federally built facility. Both bills failed, and the surprise election victory of the Democrats in 1948 slowed the effort to end preference power. The next year, however, the power companies succeeded in blocking an effort by the federal government to build its own transmission lines to carry preference power and prevailed in asserting their own right to do so. But they failed in an attempt to use their right to build transmission lines as a means of limiting the amount of preference power they were required to carry.

The industry attacks on the construction of new federal generators and on preference power often characterized such progress as communist, evoking America's enemy after World War II. Government support of an activity in which the private sector might also be involved was anathema. Soon after his 1952 election as president, Dwight Eisenhower called the TVA an example of "creeping socialism."[56] He worried that lower electric rates would attract industry from New England to the South, a transfer of economic power from a traditionally GOP area to the then-Democratic stronghold. But Eisenhower's aversion to public power meant that the government had no role to play in bringing down rates in New England, where a federal power project proposed by Roosevelt was suffering a slow death.

The issue of public power and its ability to sell electricity for less than investor-owned utilities had become a partisan battleground. Gone were the days when progressive Republicans like Senator George Norris, the TVA's principal sponsor, would be comfortable supporting Democratic initiatives to extend public power. Except for GOP members of Congress from midwestern states where public power was entrenched, the Republicans would always line up on the side of the power companies. They did not care that what they called "socialism" actually worked, producing lower cost for customers. And they would not mind providing tax breaks to the investor-owned power companies, though some called it "corporate socialism."

The Eisenhower administration's obvious sympathies with the power companies' attempt to squelch public power provided a campaign issue for John F. Kennedy in his 1960 election campaign against Eisenhower's vice president, Richard M. Nixon. The perception that the United States was falling behind the Soviet Union was the principal theme of the Kennedy campaign, and that included the Soviet lead in the construction of government-backed hydro facilities. Kennedy also criticized the Eisenhower-Nixon administration for appointments to the FPC that, he said, favored the private utilities. Eisenhower inadvertently helped Kennedy when, in 1960, he refused to reappoint an FPC commissioner, William R. Connole, because he was "identified with one particular point of view."[57] The man was too favorable to consumers.

The conflict over the use of transmission by public power soon resumed. Preference power would do the munis little good if they could not bring it from the generator to the customers. Transmission owners were free to set rates for the use of their facilities so high that municipals would lose the advantage of their access to federally generated power. That made it seem essential that the federal government itself build transmission from its own hydroelectric facilities to the preference power customers. When Kennedy brought up the Eisenhower policy in his debates with Nixon, the vice president was defensive. After Nixon's defeat and after analyzing proposals by private companies and the federal alternative, the Eisenhower administration, just before leaving office in early 1961, surprisingly opted for federally financed transmission. When the Kennedy administration took office, it wasted no time in supporting the same position. Nonetheless, partisan warfare broke out, but Kennedy said that federal financing was essential "to insure that the federal investment in these projects [transmission lines] will benefit the general public."[58] The Kennedy Administration prevailed in Congress, only to compromise with the power companies, believing that if the companies were allowed to build some of the required transmission lines, they had promised to allow access to all, and the result would be the same as if the government built them all. Stewart Udall, the Kennedy Interior Secretary who had made the deal with the power companies, later admitted that the power companies had not kept their part of the bargain and had acted in "bad faith and selfishness."[59]

But more problems were to come. In 1978, a license to build and operate a dam granted to Utah Power and Light (UP&L) was about to expire. Both UP&L and the City of Bountiful applied for the new license. Bountiful claimed that the Federal Water Power Act, though it had allowed fifty-year licenses to get generating dams built, intended that the lengthy license period would be sufficient for the investor-owned utility to earn a satisfactory return and then permit a reversion to the municipal utility's preference right of ownership. There would be no harm to the dam builder, and the expected public benefit would at last be realized. The FERC staff's position was that if either party—the investor-owned utility or public power—could manage the facility equally well, preference was the "tiebreaker." The power companies argued that preference applied only to new licenses and not to renewals. In June 1980, FERC ruled in favor of its staff position. The decision was appealed to the Eleventh Circuit Court of Appeals, which upheld FERC's opinion.

While the court proceedings moved forward, there had been a presidential election, and Republican Ronald Reagan came into office, succeeding Democrat Jimmy Carter. New commissioners now dominated FERC, and they asked the solicitor general, the federal official who argues the government's cases before the U.S. Supreme Court, to request that the Court send *Bountiful,* as the case was known, back to the commission or to the U.S. Court of Appeals. Such a request—an agency asking a court to overturn the agency's own decision that had been affirmed in a lower court—was unprecedented. The solicitor general refused to go along with this political switch. Despite the opposition of the solicitor general, FERC went to the Supreme Court on its own and asked for its own decision to be reversed. The commission clearly saw itself as a political rather than a regulatory body. In mid-1983, the Court declined this request and upheld municipal preference on relicensing.[60] In effect, it said that FERC could not change its mind in the middle of the proceeding simply because of a change in membership.

But the power companies and their Reagan administration allies were not finished fighting the war over preference. In 1982, public utility districts in Clark and Cowlitz counties in Washington State sought to acquire a license on renewal at the Merwin Dam that had been assigned to Pacific Power and Light (PP&L) but was located in their service area. In September 1983, rejecting its staff's recommendation, a FERC majority decided to reverse the *Bountiful* position and assign the license to PP&L. The commission concluded that preference applied only to original applications, meaning that once the opportunity was lost to consumer-owned utilities, it was lost forever.

The scene again shifted to the federal courts. When FERC refused to reconsider its decision in the Merwin case, the Washington counties asked the courts to review the reversal of a matter that had previously been settled in the courts in the *Bountiful* case. The principal forum was the Court of Appeals for the D.C. Circuit, the court that normally reviews federal agency decisions. A three-judge panel of the full court ruled that FERC could not reverse its interpretation of the Federal Water Power Act by challenging a matter already decided in court. FERC, now supported by the new Reagan administration and continuing on its political tack, insisted that the matter should be heard by the full Appeals Court panel.

Meanwhile, the utilities went to Congress seeking an amendment to eliminate preference power on relicensing. State regulators supported the power companies on the grounds that if investor-owned utilities lost their rights to the hydro power, their rates to their customers would increase, while the countervailing benefit to public power customers would reach fewer people. At this point, actions by the courts and the Congress intersected.

Just as membership of FERC had changed with the Reagan administration, so had the composition of the D.C. Circuit Court. The full court now included such luminaries as Ken Starr, the future Clinton Watergate prosecutor, Antonin Scalia, and Ruth Bader Ginsburg, both future Supreme Court justices, and Robert Bork, who would fail to be confirmed for a position on the high court. Having a majority made up of Reagan appointees, the court voted on a strictly partisan basis to allow FERC to reverse its position on *Bountiful* as it applied to Merwin. Starr, writing for the majority on the Court of Appeals, said that an agency could change its interpretation of the law, thus ending any hope for preference on license renewals.[61] With this decision and the opinions of their state regulators in mind, members of Congress voted overwhelmingly to eliminate any municipal preference on renewal. The issue of the Merwin Dam was left to FERC's discretion because Congress chose not to intervene in a matter so far along in the judicial process, but in fact, even that project was doomed.

The death of public preference cut public power off from what it regarded as its birthright and changed the future face of the electric industry. Where there had been the possibility that with access to increasing amounts of power supply, consumer-owned power, making use of public resources without profit, could contribute to greater consumer control of electric supply, such a possibility was dashed by the Kennedy deal with the power companies on transmission and the Reagan administration's partiality toward the power companies.

In response to these setbacks, some public power entities formed groups called joint action agencies, which enjoyed most of the same benefits as munis, to develop their own nonprofit generating plants or purchase interests in other plants. While these agencies represented a response to threats against municipal preference, they also meant that supply costs of public power would be forced up.

One major policy of the Kennedy administration was not rolled back by the Reagan administration. As captive customers, munis had been forced to pay whatever the host utilities wanted to charge for transmission, sometimes under the superficial supervision of state regulators. That changed thanks to the appointment of Joe Swidler, formerly chief counsel of the TVA, as chairman of the FPC. His appointment was a direct result of efforts by public power. After a history of being ignored or threatened by the FPC, munis would for first time be in a good position to deal with corporate power companies.

The case that turned the tide involved the Colton, California, municipal utility. State regulators had approved Southern California Edison's request for a transmission rate increase on power supplied to the muni. When Colton appealed to the FPC, the state argued that the power being supplied was not involved in interstate commerce and that the FPC must look at each transmission case individually and not assume broad jurisdiction simply because a transaction might be in interstate commerce. The FPC disagreed and took jurisdiction over transmission rates. Ultimately, the U.S. Supreme Court upheld the Swidler-led commission, saying that it could make a blanket determination that all power supply was involved in interstate commerce.[62] Munis could at last look to a neutral body to determine the fairness of wholesale rates. And even as the composition of the federal regulatory body has changed over the years, the precedents established by Swidler and his colleagues have endured.

The power companies attempted to overturn Swidler's policy by congressional action and enlisted the support of state regulators, who were losing jurisdiction over wholesale transactions. Because

of the involvement of state representatives on the side of the utilities, the companies' bill had a chance of passing. When it lost by a
single vote in the Senate Commerce Committee, the matter was
finally decided.

Untiring, the power companies keep up their pressure on the
munis. The investor-owned utilities consistently oppose the tax
treatment accorded to public power. They have focused their efforts
on both the munis' access to tax-exempt financing, which lowers
debt-service costs, and their immunity from income taxes. Of
course, as nonprofits, munis could largely avoid income taxes by
simply reducing their rates so there is nothing to tax. When owning
transmission facilities became more attractive after the passage of
EPAct, the investor-owned utilities tried to limit the ability of both
munis and co-ops to finance any new lines with the use of tax-
exempt financing. Although virtually all such efforts have failed,
the attacks continue.

The Reagan administration promoted the policy that federal
power marketing administrations, a major source of preference
power for munis, should charge market-based rates. They would
increase their rates to levels approximating the cost of power from
investor-owned utilities. While the marketing administrations did
not need to earn a return on equity because they were debt
financed, the federal entities' additional revenues from market-
based rates would immediately increase government revenues. This
appealing policy would also increase the cost of preference power,
making municipal utilities seem less attractive when compared with
the power companies. The American Public Power Association, the
public power trade association, vigorously opposed the proposal,
but the move toward a more openly competitive power market
meant that its adoption was inevitable.

The power companies give the highest priority to fighting

against the creation of any new municipal utilities. Whenever the issue is raised in a community, the local power company is free to use its shareholders' funds to launch a campaign against the initiative. The municipality, on the other hand, is almost always prevented from using taxpayer funds to promote its case. In one campaign, Miami, Florida, sought to promote a municipal utility and scheduled a referendum. All it could finance with public funds was an expert study to spotlight the savings that would result. Florida Power and Light, after refusing to supply any data for the study, waged an expensive media campaign, spending hundreds of thousands of dollars on commercials in both English and Spanish. The proposal was defeated in a landslide vote. Even in cases where industrial customers were willing to finance a campaign in favor of municipalization, they would easily be outspent by the power company. In recent decades, virtually no new munis have been created.

One area where public power saw an opportunity was Montana, where the state's major investor-owned utility had self-destructed after restructuring was launched. Five municipalities created Montana Public Power Inc. to make an unsolicited bid to acquire the remnants of the utility. In 2005, the battle was joined with investors who wanted to keep the company private.

Public power has seen itself as the benchmark by which the industry should be measured. The result should be lower rates for customers. But the industry record is of persistent efforts to erase the benchmark so that power companies will have no standard of comparison. Even based on the best intentions, the new power market has done much to eliminate opportunities for public power to show its value. Instead of low-cost electricity from public power, the solution was to be the market. One works; the other has not.

The public power battles of the past sixty years are a curious piece of industry history. Where consumers, acting through local government, have chosen to establish their own utility rather than relying on one owned by investors, they have almost invariably obtained electric service at costs far below those of the investor-owned utility. Public power provides service of equal reliability. Yet munis have been forced to fight against efforts by power companies and government to put them out of business simply because they are not owned by investors, earning profits and paying taxes. An idea that works and has been proven over time must struggle against forces whose success means higher costs for consumers. These municipal utilities have existed as long as the power companies. If nothing else, public power is a survivor.

Cooperatives Fill a Gap

Rural electrification cooperatives were part of the New Deal initiative that led to the creation of the Rural Electrification Administration (REA), later renamed the Rural Utilities Service to reflect its involvement in telecommunications as well as electricity. In rural areas with no electric service, the federal government urged people to gather support for the creation of co-ops, utilities owned by their members. The Roosevelt administration wanted to lift the standard of living across the country, and rural development had been hampered by a nineteenth-century energy system. Once a local effort was launched, the REA would provide low-cost, long-term loans for distribution lines to be built connecting the co-op's customers to the grid and bringing power from generators, often those at federal dams. Because there would be only a few customers for each mile of line, a co-op could be costly, justifying the low-cost loans. The co-op, like the muni, is debt financed, although a small fee by each co-op member counts as customer-contributed capital and forms the co-op's capital base in addition to the co-op's retained earnings.

The co-ops, now numbering 885 and operating in all but three states, accomplished their purpose in bringing electric service to the sparsely populated areas of the entire country. Their achievement was based on a grassroots effort, unusual in the evolution of the business, during the 1930s and 1940s. As a result, many members felt a strong sense of commitment to their utility. While co-op rates were often high, despite the low-cost debt, the customers were grateful for the access they had gained.

The heady days of fighting to create rural utilities have vanished. The federal government's low-cost lending has decreased to the point where it offers rates tied to the municipal and other markets. Co-ops now use other financial institutions or go directly to the market. Standard & Poor's, which analyzes borrowers' finances, now warns that co-ops will have "to achieve greater margins to meet stronger credit metrics," language that could apply to investor-owned utilities.

Not only would their unique form of financing have to change to become more like those of other utilities, but their markets would also change. No longer would co-ops be the only way that many rural areas could hope to get electricity; investor-owned utilities have broadened their view and are ready to reach out to and hold rural customers. And many of the co-ops' territories have also changed. Said one observer: "While cooperatives are rural entities, the transformation of agricultural areas into suburban settings is noticeable."[63]

From their idealistic, customer-driven origins, co-ops have evolved into utilities indistinguishable in many ways from the investor-owned utilities that actively serve rural customers. Even before restructuring, some co-ops had created their own generation alternatives. Besides the distribution co-ops, many of them quite small, scores of generation and transmission co-ops were created.

Their members are other co-ops, not individuals. These wholesale co-ops are part of the answer to the gradual loss of preference power for which co-ops had become eligible in the 1940s.

The co-ops are private, independent, electric utility businesses. The heads of co-ops, formerly known as general managers, might now be known as chief executive officers, but the co-ops are not investor-owned, at least in the usual sense. Because they are consumer-owned utilities, they remain unregulated in most states and by FERC—and they fight hard to retain that status. Although they are nonprofit, they may choose to invest their retained earnings in ways similar to investor-owned utilities, including in unrelated businesses. As a result, economies they achieve may result not in lower rates but in funds for further business expansion. And the co-ops often resist efforts to force them to allow their retail customers access to competitive power supply, just as do the most hidebound investor-owned utilities.

What distinguishes cooperatives from investor-owned utilities and even from many municipal utilities is the direct election of the board by the co-op's members. But the enthusiasm of the early years has given way to the same customer indifference experienced by other utilities. Many co-ops have to struggle and even give cash awards to get enough members to come out and vote. The greatest strength of the co-op—its commitment to "democratic member control"—is increasingly a myth.

Despite the start of wholesale access to transmission, co-op members have seen little positive effect. The retention of gains for other business purposes, the availability of power supply from generation and transmission entities that distribution co-ops are committed to support, and the co-ops' reluctance to allow their customers access to the open market all work against the expressed intent of EPAct. Yet co-ops continue to play a valuable role in many areas.

Like other utilities, the co-ops have formed a powerful trade organization, the National Rural Electric Cooperative Association (NRECA), a political force that often makes far more political contributions than any individual investor-owned utility but with much the same pattern and intent. In 2004, it gave $1,503,000, with 55 percent going to Republicans.[64] It not only lobbies for co-ops but provides a broad basket of services enabling them to operate with the advantages available to much larger utilities, ranging from billing to engineering advice. As federal loan money has been cut back, reflecting the success of the effort to bring power to rural America, NRECA has developed its own financial arm, raising money in the financial markets to loan to co-ops, sometimes as a supplement to federal loans, which themselves now mimic market rates. NRECA makes a major contribution to keeping co-ops immune from efforts by investor-owned utilities to absorb them. Its lobbying efforts in Washington are aimed at keeping co-ops unregulated. In response to the 2005 energy law, which preserved the independence of co-ops but backed huge federal handouts to the big industry players and killed PUHCA, NRECA virtually gushed in appreciation, thanking Congress for "ultimately recognizing and protecting the right of consumers to own and operate their independent electric cooperatives."[65] The independence of co-ops was worth the potentially higher cost of power. Over the years, in part because of their less desirable market areas and in part because of their strong lobbying effort, the co-ops have had fewer difficulties with the power companies and the government than have the munis.

Only the consumers served by munis and co-ops enjoy the opportunity of getting the kind of utility service they want, because they own the utility and do not have to accommodate shareholder requirements.

Consumer Advocacy Arrives

In most states, the utility regulatory body has traditionally designated a part of its staff to represent the consumer interest in rate
cases. As a result, the regulatory staff would be split between
people advising the regulators and others who, though also serving
on the commission staff, argue as if they were independent lawyers.
Often a person might play one of these roles in a case and then shift
to the other role in a second case. The staff members representing
consumer interests seldom consult with the people they represent.
Only when a consumer group, such as an industrial association or
the AARP, appears in a proceeding, do the staff and the customer
representatives make contact.

Sensing a political opportunity, state attorneys general began
designating part of their staffs to intervene in regulatory proceedings. At first, such involvement was more a gesture than a coherent
effort to represent customer interests. In the 1970s, just as electric
rates began to climb, state governments began to show interest in
providing a formal means of representing consumer interests. All
but a handful of states now have either a consumer advocate office
or[2] similar agency or a much-strengthened and better-funded role
for the attorney general's office.

Consumer advocates have usually focused on cases in which rates
would be set. Their goal has been to persuade utility regulators to
look more closely at the utilities' requests and to pare down the proposed rate increase. They often measure their success in terms of the
reduction in the amount of rate relief ultimately granted to the utilities. This approach is understandable, because customers are concerned above all with their monthly bill. The results, while
appreciable, hardly produce rates as low as the munis have.

Less than half the states provide funding above $1 million for the
operation of their advocacy staffs. In all but half a dozen states, the

advocacy agency's funding is only a small fraction of the funds given to the regulators and tiny when compared with what the utilities spend on litigation.

Perhaps the ultimate irony is how consumers finance both sides in regulatory proceedings. The amount of funding, either from a utility rate surcharge or from taxpayers, that goes to consumer advocacy offices is set by legislatures, and some advocates are supported by voluntary contributions. These funds come from customers, the people represented. Utilities have the right to include their regulatory costs in their cost of service. While state commissions can review such costs, they are usually not examined closely and are almost automatically passed on to customers. Customers end up paying for both their representation, which seeks to keep their rates down, and that of the utilities, which seeks to increase consumers' rates, resulting in investment returns for their shareholders. And customers usually spend more on supporting the utilities' interest than on their own. This situation provides an incentive for utilities to spend all they can to win and for spending on customer advocacy to be restrained, because customers must foot the whole bill.

Legislative miserliness with consumer representatives suggests that government is often trying to improve its own image without seriously challenging the utilities. As consumer representation has increased, the traditional use of the regulatory staff to represent customers has withered in some states. The result may well be that in many states, with the introduction of more visible consumer advocates and the elimination of the commission staff role, the amount of public resources devoted to representing customers has actually been reduced.

The fifty states and the District of Columbia spend less than $100 million a year on consumer representatives.[66] That is likely to be less than a single national utility, such as the Southern Company or

Duke or Exelon, is likely to spend on legislative and regulatory activities in a single year. With such limited funding, there is little that a consumer advocate can do but react to rate filings by the utilities. Consumer advocates claim credit, with sound justification in most cases, for getting regulators to reduce requested rate increases, but their victories are more a matter of degree than a reversal of the relentless demand of the industry for the right to collect more revenues. Occasions when current rates are cut back because of consumer advocate action are rare and can be considered major wins.

Like utility regulators, consumer offices lack the funds to hire competent experts capable of matching the utilities' own employees and able to dig into utility operations. They cannot challenge the utility's cost of service and must frequently choose only a portion of the utility's case on which to focus their limited resources. Resolutions on electric industry restructuring adopted by the National Association of Utility Consumer Advocates have had no measurable impact because the lobbying resources of consumer advocates are minuscule compared with those of the major utilities.

The growth of state consumer representation has provided customers a voice in the regulatory process, a system generally stacked against them, and consumer advocate agencies have been joined by voluntary groups such as AARP, but such groups also have only limited resources to devote to participating in state proceedings. Consumer advocates can remind the commissions and legislators of how decisions affect end users, but their voice is weak, and their gains are limited.

While the growth of consumer representation has spread across the states, no similar development had occurred at the federal level. In part because FERC regulation takes place at least one step removed from the end-use customer, consumers have never gained institutional representation in its proceedings. Within FERC there is virtually no pretense that customers' interests are to be protected, because the commission does not see itself as a regulator of utility operations directly responsible for end-use customers. In adhering to the view that its scope extends only to the players in the wholesale market, FERC apparently assumes that the wholesale customers, even if they are investor-owned utilities, will take care of the interests of their own customers. Lack of representation of consumer interests at FERC produces results based on the presumption that regulatory paternalism is sufficient. And state regulators must simply pass through to customers the costs resulting from FERC orders.

In 2002, two of Oregon's congressional representatives proposed legislation to create a federal energy consumer advocate and suggested that it be made part of the pending energy bill. The Enron collapse and chaos in FERC's handling of mounting costs to customers led to these demands from Oregon, which was directly affected by Enron's manipulation. The proposal called for an advocate to deal not only with FERC matters but those of regional transmission organizations. The proposal received little attention in Congress, and when the energy bill was passed three years later, there was no mention of consumer representation.

Utilities and Their Trade Associations

APPA: American Public Power Association, the association of municipal utilities and public utility districts.

Cooperative (co-op): A rural electric cooperative owned by its members and serving as a local electric utility, usually in a sparsely populated area. Governed by an elected Board of Directors.

COUs: Consumer-owned utilities, nonprofit entities, including cooperatives, munis, and public utility districts, that are mostly financed by borrowing.

EEI: Edison Electric Association, the trade group of investor-owned utilities.

G&Ts: Generation and transmission cooperatives that supply distribution co-ops.

IOUs: Investor-owned utilities, for-profit entities serving as local electric utilities.

Joint Action Agencies: Generators that are developed by groups of municipals and that supply their member utilities.

Munis: Municipal electric utilities, affiliated with municipalities and governed by elected or appointed boards.

NRECA: National Rural Electric Cooperative Association, representing cooperatives. Also provides central services to members.

CHAPTER 10

THE NEXT ROUND OF REFORM

From Edison to Enron and beyond, the increasing use of electricity in America has been more about the producers and purveyors than about the consumers. In the early days, people quickly came to depend on lightbulbs and electric motors, and when electricity represented only a small part of the family budget or the cost of industrial production, its cost raised no concerns. When it was still a miracle of science, its lack of reliability was acceptable.

The big companies that made and sold electric power were left to do as they wished.

As consumers began to take electricity for granted, the power companies began to take the consumers for granted. Electricity became a necessity of life. Consumers became dependent not only on electricity but on electric utilities.

Except for the administration of Franklin D. Roosevelt, government did little to protect consumers. Regulators failed to protect them. Both legislators and regulators have fallen into the habit of telling consumers that by paying more now, they will pay less later. The promises of government pave the path to disappointment in electricity as in most other matters.

Today, the big companies that make and sell electric power are left to do as they wish. "The more things change, the more they remain the same."

Consumers want what they have always been promised: reliable service at the lowest reasonable price.

The electric utility industry needs reform if it is to meet consumers' needs. Such reform can take place without revolution and while respecting the ways in which the industry has evolved. A true electric industry restructuring should focus on four areas: the market, transmission, public policy, and enhancing the role of the consumer.

SIMPLIFYING THE MARKET

The electric utility market, which was supposed to open up because of the Energy Policy Act of 1992, has almost completely failed. Although operators in trading rooms and control rooms carry out transactions between buyers and sellers, the consumer has yet to see any real change except increased cost. The market itself cannot eliminate the costs of paying off old utility failures or of new fuel price increases. The market itself cannot prevent fraud, so the reaction to Enron continues to ripple across all aspects of the business. The market requires less blind faith in its value and greater care devoted to its development.

1. Competition should be focused on the wholesale market

The basic rule of EPAct—limiting the requirement of open transmission access and competitive markets to the wholesale business—
is the correct first step. Buyers and sellers are more sophisticated
and capable of defending themselves in a wholesale market setting.
The lessons learned in the wholesale market can later be extended
into retail. A large share of the financial benefits to be derived by
customers from competition can come from a purely wholesale
market. And the wholesale market has barely begun to be launched
in many areas; work remains to be done in an immature business.

Some states have already adopted retail access, even going to the
point of requiring utilities to divest themselves of generation. Obviously, these divestitures cannot be undone, and each state will pro-
ceed as it chooses. But it is possible to retreat from unworkable
programs in which the state must mandate prices. The best state
plan for those that have gone too far simply to abandon retail access
is the Maine model, where all customers obtain competitive power,
even those still taking the default service.

2. The development of the electricity market should be gradual, and market rules should be simple

FERC and some states have tried to develop fully articulated market
rules without a good understanding of how the market for this unique
product would work. The desire to produce positive results quickly,
whatever the mistakes, is the key reason that industry restructuring
has achieved almost no appreciable benefit for consumers.

The electricity market should be allowed to develop as have
other markets—gradually and reflecting the participants' needs.
Regulators should no longer prescribe the products to be traded but
should allow players to trade whatever suits the customers,

including full bundled services composed of both generation and transmission. Transactions should be of whatever length customers demand, from day-ahead to decade-ahead.

The bilateral market, where deals are made directly between seller and buyer, should no longer be discouraged. It is not up to regulators to set the price signals that customers ought to receive; let them choose what they want. Forcing transactions into "gross" deals rather than allowing bilateral arrangements to be supplemented by "net" transactions makes no economic sense and may work against the interests of both the buyer and the seller.

Allowing more "organic" market development may result in an understanding of distribution of risk different from the century-long practice in the industry. Even in the developing electricity market since 1992, risk almost invariably continues to find its way to the customer. In a market setting, there is no reason for the continuance of the rules applied to the erstwhile monopolies to determine who bears the risk. In short, sellers need to be ready to accept risk. Fuel price increases should not be almost automatically and entirely passed on to customers.

Where there has been little restructuring, and utilities have remained as unbundled as they were before EPAct, they have made a choice and should not be immune from accepting some risk. Similarly, when a utility is merely passing through the cost of power supply obtained from generators it does not own, price risk should not be imposed solely on the end-use customer; the generator should be responsible.

The complexity and related administrative costs of ISOs and similar bodies have been among the chief obstacles to an active market. These bodies impose too great a burden on potential players, who have to invest heavily in compliance and in managing market operations. This burden has favored the largest companies and discouraged or eliminated smaller competitors. A thriving market depends on active competition and customer choice. The potential for such a market has been barred by the obstacles constructed in the name of its creation. Too many rules have led to too few competitors.

If the electricity market is allowed to evolve in line with the needs and desires of the participants, it will need far fewer market rules to prescribe the details of its operations. Markets can adopt their own rules subject to regulatory approval.

3. FERC and other regulators should not issue market mandates but should control the actions of market players other than generators and customers

Electric utility regulation has departed from its traditional and necessary role of restraining and governing the behavior of the participants under its jurisdiction. It now seeks to make choices on behalf of customers and to channel behavior to suit its vision of the market. This new style of regulation has produced an excessive assertion of authority but no good results.

The principal benefit of restructuring has been to relieve customers of responsibility for generators. The mistakes of bundled utilities, in the form of stranded costs, are gradually fading. If restructuring means anything at all, customers should never have to take generation risk and face the possibility of paying for power plants that do not work. FERC will undermine the only discernable value resulting so far from restructuring if it imposes on customers any artificial costs of generation. It should refrain from doing so.

In the same spirit, regulators should not arbitrarily increase prices as a way of increasing the opportunities for competitive suppliers. Competition is not the end purpose of the market; it is only of value if it can produce lower prices. Raising prices to achieve competition simply gets a basic law of economics backwards.

Because industry restructuring is not deregulation, regulators still have a role. They must continue to control monopolies. Equally important, they must police and root out market abuses. The principles of American antitrust law are sound, but they have not been applied rigorously. With the end of the monopoly generation regime, regulators have an enhanced responsibility to take on these tasks and give them high priority. There has been too much attention to market rules and too little to consumer protection.

4. Regulatory commissions should be given better staffs

Utilities produce information or misinformation, and regulators consume both. Commissions, both federal and state, lack the ability to scrutinize the operations of the entities they regulate. A utility's cost of service—the basis for the rates it is authorized to collect—is composed of thousands of items, but regulators review only a few and accept most of what they are told. When regulators undertake a rare management audit of a utility, the standard is usually the behavior of other utilities, not the behavior of the private sector as a whole. The consumer, who pays both the regulatory cost and the utility bill, is shortchanged.

Regulatory bodies need to have staff trained in all aspects of utility operations and financed sufficiently to keep companies under virtually continuous review. In particular, both federal and state regulatory bodies need more engineering staff.

Congress has now determined that the ERO will be subject to FERC supervision. Because the ERO grows out of a utility-run organization, controls will be needed to insure that cost-effective standards are both put in place and managed strictly. FERC needs to have more technical staff for this purpose.

Regulators should also be able to insure that risk management tools are financially realistic and should have the right to regulate their soundness. They should also be able to determine that suppliers have the financial and technical ability to keep their commitments, whatever their market-based deals may be.

5. Markets should be regional, not national

Experience has shown that one size does not fit all. Setting requirements for a national market because such a market would encourage competitors seems only to allow large utilities to have the opportunity to dominate the entire country. The resistance of New England and New York to the kind of homogenization promoted by FERC should send a message; so should the reaction of states in the Pacific Northwest to SMD. A vast country is not fertile ground for a mandated national market.

Greatly simplified market rules will encourage competitors far more than a national market. In fact, some smaller entities might choose to tailor their activities to smaller markets. Experience gained in regional markets, where the players have preexisting patterns of cooperation, may possibly lead to broader markets. As with market rules, it would be preferable to allow regions and markets to develop naturally rather than imposing direction from above.

6. Electricity products should be customer-driven, not dictated by regulators

The naturally developing market is likely to supply products customers want. Markets should allow for variation in price, the composition of bundled products, lengths of contracts, degrees of reliability and risk, sensitivity to changing supply costs, and any other factors that buyers and sellers define. Legislators and regulators will learn more about what the market needs and how it can best be controlled.

States where there is retail competition must continue to provide a default service. This service should be available to those who make no market choice and to provide protection against the failure of a supplier to meet its commitments. (In the wholesale market, customers should be responsible for finding their own protection.) There is no reason to force people into making choices they do not want to make.

The case for default service results from other recommendations: no artificial pricing, natural development of the market, and keeping the market simple.

Because suppliers do not want to seek out small customers one by one, and because consumers have made it clear they have no interest in shopping for electricity, the best-functioning purchasing group is composed of those customers accepting default power. If the industry and, more important, regulators give people what they want—to play only a passive role—then default power, sometimes called "the standard offer," will probably be a permanent part of the market system.

Transmission: Key to the Market

A major development in the evolution of the electricity business was the recognition that transmission must be a common carrier; as such, it would be the key to creation of an open market. But the industry has not made good on the promise of open access to transmission. For the wholesale market to function effectively, transmission and generation must be separated. If the transmission owner controls access and pricing on the transmission system, it can inevitably favor its own generation.

7. Independent management and ownership of the transmission system are essential

The law requires that wholesale access be available in any state. That means that any reseller—an investor-owned or a consumer-owned utility—should be able to be reached by all suppliers on a basis that does not discriminate against the independent supplier in favor of the incumbent host utility.

Independent management means more than the formality of the technicians who accept transmission reservations or maintain reliable operations being separated from the rest of the utility. The policy of requiring a separation between employees of a single company carrying supposedly independent functions creates only an illusion of transmission independence. These paper "walls" are not monitored, and customers have no way of knowing whether they have been breached. The system needs to be managed and upgraded under management that is not beholden to the shareholders of the company owning the generation. Otherwise, as a company employee, the transmission operator is bound to serve the company's owners.

This separation is critically important where utilities remain vertically integrated and especially where there is no retail access. While customers may get low prices from the maintenance of the utility regime as it existed before restructuring, they deserve the opportunity to have the market tested by forcing the utilities to consider purchased-power options in preference to their own resources. Giving outside suppliers the opportunity to enter the service territory of an unbundled utility may not change anything, but it enhances the possibility of choice.

The recently adopted principle that the traditional supplier has special rights to the use of transmission to serve its native load is misguided and insures that competition has no chance of success. Even allowing the host utility to provide default service incurs some risk, but allowing it a preferential position on its own system almost certainly negates customer choice. Instead of permitting this preference, Congress needs to reverse course and amend this obvious gift to the utilities at the potential expense of their customers. The provision is a prime example of the kind of outdated paternalism practiced by legislatures, regulators, and utilities.

In promoting open access, FERC embarked on the most positive method for dealing with the need to end the linkage between supply and transmission when it began to promote ITCs. Insuring ownership of the grid by regulated companies having no other interest beyond increasing its use is the best way of assuring that transmission owners cannot exploit the lines to promote their own generation. These companies derive their profit from the traffic on their wires.

ITCs are preferable to ISOs and RTOs, though they would serve the same purpose. ISOs have no incentive to build new transmission when needed and instead come up with costly solutions like LICAP, a measure that would eviscerate a core purpose of restructuring—the goal of removing generator risk from customers. ITCs, which are rate-regulated but have a profit motive, would be able to move directly to deal with transmission bottlenecks and would avoid costly and ineffective generator incentives.

Reliance on nonprofit ISOs, rather than ITCs that have their investment on the line, promotes irresponsible behavior, according to Greg Williams, a former FERC staff attorney who is now a leading practitioner before the Commission. Under the 2005 law, an ISO may be found to have violated reliability standards. Because ISOs are supported by customers, the cost of any penalties would be passed on to the same customers who suffered the outages caused by the ISOs' violations. Unless transmission operators have a financial stake in the business, the customers have to pay. With ITCs, the shareholders would pay.

As ITCs began to be developed, they offered a fair buyout to current owners, and they capped rates. FERC was reluctant to allow them attractive rates of return even if such returns would not affect the user rates. But owners would sell only if pressed by FERC, for they realized that the grid would provide them both the ability to dominate their own customers and a solid revenue stream. FERC ultimately backed off because of utility opposition.

The 2005 energy law allows rates of return on transmission to be set at more attractive levels to promote the construction of new lines. While this provision of the law should encourage ITCs, it probably will not do so. Instead the current utility transmission owners will gain more profit for doing what they should have done without such returns.

The government cannot order utilities to sell their transmission to independent owners. But FERC can resume the pursuit of its former policy of pressing for complete separation of transmission from other utility operations and favoring independent ownership. In view of utility concerns about loss of profits from these lines, the utilities can be passive, minority owners while the independent investors select the management of the lines.

The independent ownership of the transmission grid, regulated by the use of performance-based rates, is the best assurance of common-carrier transmission, the essential element of competition. It should be pursued.

8. Transmission reliability deserves the highest priority

There is no excuse for human error causing the kind of massive blackouts that were experienced in 1965 and 2003. For the first time, federal regulators have the authority and responsibility to prevent catastrophic blackouts.

FERC should require that the ERO get effective standards in place at the earliest possible date. FERC must monitor ERO performance closely, and both agencies must monitor ISOs and transmission owners. It is too late to take information on faith or to make unverified assumptions about transmission operations.

Two practical measures may be indicated. First, the ERO should make unannounced on-site inspections of ISOs and utility control rooms. If bank examiners can make such inspections of all financial institutions, the ERO should do no less. This is a matter of homeland security. Second, all transmission operators and ISO managers should be licensed by FERC or the ERO, just as those working at nuclear power plants are licensed by the Nuclear Regulatory Commission. Poor performance by key operating personnel at the outset of the blackout of 2003 showed that their competence cannot be left solely under the control of the transmission owner or ISO management, when the consequences of their actions can be so widespread.

PUBLIC POLICY: UPDATE FOR THE TIMES

As utility policy at the national level has undergone significant changes, state policy has lagged or has even served to undermine the potential for competitive benefit for consumers. The federal government seems to have become the compliant tool of the major power companies, while the states have either acquiesced or been overridden. State legislative reforms are needed.

9. States should have energy policies

After years of struggle without success, the federal government adopted its version of an energy policy in 2005. This federal action does not represent a coherent view of energy policy except for the one consistent element: using tax subsidies to encourage energy-related investments.

In the years since the crises of the 1970s, states have generally retreated from significant energy policies. While some states continue to promote conservation, their programs are usually the remnants of more aggressive measures adopted during previous price run-ups. They are faced again with increases in fuel costs and utility bills with few tools to deal with them.

State energy policies need to address objectives designed to benefit consumers, support the economy, and promote efficiency. Because of the lack of a comprehensive federal approach, the difficulties in restructuring the electricity market, the likelihood that fuel prices will remain high, and the long hiatus since the states reviewed their policies, action by the states is now urgently needed. There are limits on what can be accomplished at the state level, but strong action in key states can set the pattern for other states, even for federal action. And states can choose to work together as they have on environmental matters.

10. End social policy and other government mandates financed by electric bill surcharges

The practice of adding surcharges to electric bills to finance public policy initiatives should be ended, and existing charges should be repealed. If the country is supposed to be moving toward the treatment of electricity as a product subject to competitive forces, tacking on charges to support social programs and other legislative mandates is both contradictory and misguided.

There have been two reasons for these add-ons. First, legislatures look for ways to raise revenues without raising taxes, providing public support to those struggling to pay energy bills. Most public assistance, including payments to cover heating oil, comes from general tax revenues, but because electric rates are regulated, electricity customers are singled out to pay the costs of universal service and related programs to help low-income consumers pay their light bills. This policy is unwise and unfair.

A second basis for mandated surcharges on electric bills has been the belief held by many legislators that power costs were going to decline, hiding from consumers a small addition to a declining bill. Apart from the cynicism of this policy, which would take back some of what government had just given, it obviously has not worked for electricity, though it may have done so for telephone service. Electric bills have not declined, especially as the cost of fuel has climbed.

Electric bill surcharges are bad public policy. They help legislatures shirk their responsibilities. Consumers are exploited, this time by their government.

11. States should leave pricing to the market or traditional regulation

In many states, legislatures have intervened in the regulatory process to impose on the electricity market pricing that does not reflect the way the market, regulated or competitive, is working. While government has rarely been given the authority to set prices of products in a competitive market, it may do so when it comes to prices in monopoly situations. Obviously, that is the reason for utility regulation: the purpose is to substitute careful regulatory judgment for the role that competition would otherwise play.

But it is pure politics when a legislature sets the price for power at an arbitrary level that represents a price it wants the market to produce, whether or not the market does so. Setting the price that utilities may charge to reflect the expected reductions that would result from competition is a mistake, one that should not be continued. The actual cost must be paid, and setting it artificially low means only that the difference is deferred. The legislature requires the utility to borrow funds to cover its shortfall and then to recover those funds and the interest on them from a later generation of customers. Such decisions are made without any evidence that prices will later decline and make it easy to pay the deferred costs.

The concept of deferred benefit has become an unfortunate part of the electric utility business. The problem is that today's payments are certain and tomorrow's benefits are not. High PURPA prices were set, but fuel prices did not increase enough to justify them. Long-term recovery of short-term fuel costs was adopted, but fuel costs kept increasing, so deferring their costs only made them more expensive when interest charges were taken into account. Later, legislatures believed that consumers needed to be reassured about the effects of restructuring and that mandating lower rates would provide that reassurance, but competition did not produce lower costs, leaving customers to cover the shortfall. The results of all these initiatives have been higher prices for consumers.

Trying to capture the effect of future price changes by artificially setting current prices, either high or low, does not work. Legislative price setting should be abandoned.

Perhaps even more pernicious are efforts by legislatures and regulators to use electric utility pricing to produce specific results in the market. Consumer costs should be kept as low as possible. Artificially raising these prices to make it easier for higher-cost suppliers to participate in the market is absurd. There is no likelihood that prices for consumers will ultimately fall if this policy is followed. The best that can be expected is high-cost competition.

Marketers continue to argue that some suppliers, especially unbundled utilities, disguise some of their costs to make their cost of generation look low. They propose that the generation price should be arbitrarily increased by the amount of the supposed hidden costs. Of course, they expect that the higher price will help get their products into the market. If the marketers are right, properly staffed regulators should be able to investigate and determine if such subsidies exist. Federal and state regulators should have the authority to insure that competition is fair. Presumably, such inquiries would be needed only for regulated entities, because independent generators could not have any such hidden advantages.

Above all, it is more important to protect the consumer from unnecessarily high costs than to protect the marketer from perceived hidden subsidies. If the net result of the exercise is simply to increase consumer costs, regulators must determine if short-term benefits are likely and if not, choose the solution with the lowest current cost.

Price fixing and cost deferral turn out to be the best arguments for maintaining the unbundled utility in the barely open market. Customers of the Southern Company are far more likely to approve of their electric rates than are the customers of a company with mandated high rates designed to encourage competition. The first have been spared from the competitive market, and the latter have been overdosed with it.

12. Conservation pricing should be used to support energy efficiency and renewable-fuel generation

Energy policies frequently assume that any shortage of supply is temporary. New oil and gas will be found when new wells are drilled. The dollar will get stronger. We have enough fuel—it is just a matter of building more refineries or more tankers. All these assumptions lull Americans into believing they need do nothing to use energy more efficiently. In the wake of the disastrous Hurricane Katrina in 2005, when oil wells and refineries were put out of service, President George W. Bush called for conservation, something he had not done previously. Conservation is for crises, it seems, and does not deal with the underlying fact that most fuels are being depleted, including those used to generate electricity.

The most important single force causing electricity prices to increase is the cost of fuel for generation. The Carter administration was the most mindful of the impact of rising fuel prices and instituted substantial programs to stimulate and support conservation. The hundreds of millions of dollars Carter spent or stimulated to be spent are now part of well-insulated buildings and insulation of electric water heaters. But as Americans became accustomed to higher prices and as oil prices sagged for a few years, the United States boosted its energy requirements.

Electricity consumption continues to increase. In 2005, the International Energy Agency forecast that world consumption will double in the next twenty years, and emerging economies will account for at least half of that rise. Competition for the finite supply of fuel will become more intense, and the availability of supply to meet such a sustained growth in demand is in doubt. Fuel stocks will not last forever, and as fuel grows scarce, it will grow more expensive. While it may be possible to make coal and nuclear power safer and more environmentally acceptable, conservation should be a permanent part of energy policy.

Only one conservation measure has been shown to work effectively and with certainty—higher prices. Federal funds are generally spent to encourage production, a policy that rewards producers but encourages increased consumption. More attention should be focused on the same kind of major financial support for the development of renewable resources, which are not otherwise competitive, and more efficient use of energy. The revenues needed to support these efforts should come from a surcharge applied to the use of all energy, including electricity.

From time to time, proposals are made to increase gasoline taxes by 50 cents a gallon for this purpose, but they are rejected because of the expected consumer outcry and the hardship higher prices would cause. Yet the 2004 to 2005 gasoline price run-up did not begin to have an impact on user habits and consumption until the price sharply increased by more than $1 a gallon. Prices need to be high enough to reduce consumption, but a surcharge should be instituted only if the funds are immediately and directly applied to putting renewables into the market and to greater efficiency. If the federal government can mandate low-water-use toilets, as it has, it can mandate and support low-electricity-use appliances. The federal water-saving mandate finally caused plumbing appliance makers to come up with a low-water-use toilet that works. The same can happen in energy conservation.

If such a policy is adopted, three elements are essential. First, the uses of the funds derived from a conservation surcharge should be designated beforehand, so there is no lag between raising the revenues and their producing results. This requirement would avoid the defects of policies that raise current prices on the promise of future benefit. Second, this surcharge should apply to all energy uses, not just those that are subject to regulation. In this respect it would be a tax, not a rate add-on. While this proposal may seem to contradict the need to avoid surcharges, it may be distinguished by its universal application and its being tied to immediate rather than deferred benefits. Third, as will be discussed below, the funds to develop, own, and operate new generation should be made available as explicit payments to public entities, including public power, not tax breaks for private corporations. Distributed generation—small generators producing both heat and electricity for apartment buildings and hospitals—makes sense and completely avoids the need for utilities; local governments can manage the programs on a nonprofit basis. By contrast, current policies provide assurance of only one thing— increased profits—without guaranteeing the policy goals of more production. Remove the profit motive and monitor how the funds are spent, and the effort is more likely to achieve the goals.

13. The relationship between federal and state regulation of the electric industry should be reformed, and a new form of regulation should be adopted

While the regulation of electric utilities began as a matter of state jurisdiction exclusively, in recent years FERC has been given increasing authority at the expense of state commissions. This development became especially evident after Congress mandated transmission access for wholesale transactions. FERC wasted little time in declaring that when a state opened retail access, the federal rules would automatically apply. In the 2005 energy legislation, Congress both conferred additional jurisdiction on FERC and directed state commissions to take certain actions. The ultimate imposition of federal regulation on the states on matters relating to electricity seems likely.

This trend has been invited to a considerable degree by state inaction. As transmission has increasingly been placed under the control of regional ISOs, states have not been able to deal with the local consequences, and their control over electric utilities has become less relevant. In 1973, a National Governors Association study laid out the case for states to work together to create regional regulatory bodies, because electric utility matters were already beginning to reveal that states would not be able to deal with the industry by acting individually. States rejected such an approach at that time because they were unwilling to cede any authority to regional boards. Since then, FERC has filled the gap, and ISOs, the regional operators of transmission systems, have become in effect FERC's regional regulatory subsidiaries. Unlike state or regional regulators, ISOs operate without much sense of accountability.

It is too late for states to try to take the actions suggested in 1973, because the federal government has moved on to assume more authority. The evolution of regulatory control toward the federal level has the unfortunate consequence of reducing consumer protection. While state regulators encounter the views of participants representing customer groups and of state consumer advocates, FERC is removed from such influences.

The 2005 energy law envisages a degree of common FERC and state consideration of electricity issues but at a consultative level at best; FERC retains complete authority. This law should be improved upon by requiring that jurisdiction be given to joint federal-state boards, each responsible for an area covered by a single ISO or equivalent body. Such boards could be composed of three FERC commissioners and two state regulators, chosen by all of the state commissioners in the designated area. This structure would continue FERC control, recognizing both that transmission is part of interstate commerce and that the market and access to it are under federal control. At the same time, it would recognize that regional differences exist and ought to be respected, not ignored as FERC has tried to do in recent years. And because of their being closer to the consumer, state regulators could help assure that consumer concerns are considered. If these joint boards were to hold their sessions in the regions and not in Washington, the likelihood of direct consumer involvement would be greater.

In those states that have been most resistant to change—where retail access does not exist, and wholesale access is limited by native-load preference and barely independent transmission management—joint boards could play a role by bringing the federal regulators into the regions. FERC might become more sensitive to and informed about the situation in these regions and more aware of necessary measures to open access. Washington is simply at too Olympian a height to deal with these matters.

As the electric industry has been restructured, regulatory change has been limited to lodging more authority at the federal level. It is time for a more creative and appropriate restructuring of regulation.

HELP FOR THE CONSUMER

Throughout the history of the electric industry, utilities and regulators have failed to focus on providing reliability and low prices to consumers. This failure results directly from the inability of consumers to present their case. This lack of effective representation of the consumer interest has resulted in an industry that exploits its market while coming up short on meeting its needs. The consumer interest should be better represented.

14. Public power should be supported by government action

Public power works. America's municipal utilities produce lower-cost power at least as reliably as investor-owned utilities. They have been doing this for as long as the profit-making utilities have.

Persistent opposition to the further development of public power and efforts to pare away its competitive advantages sustain the great myth that Sam Insull invented. Electricity is not a monopoly, not only because Congress discovered that fact in 1978, but because municipal utilities have existed within the territories of the larger investor-owned utilities and have consistently produced better results than they have. Consumer-owned utilities were once called a "historical accident," as though the move toward investor-owned utilities was ordained by history. Dwight Eisenhower, a president with absolutely no knowledge of the evolution of the industry, called the TVA "creeping socialism." Such statements represent the survival of the view that Edison's Pearl Street Station and the light-bulb itself would not have happened without private investment and that this natural order must remain indefinitely.

While there can be no doubt that the strength of the American economy has resulted from the free-enterprise system, where innovation and risk-taking stand to be rewarded by profit, such a conclusion cannot be so absolute that other workable approaches must be ruled out.

The private sector has traditionally asserted that public power works because of its access to preference power and because it can borrow in the tax-exempt financial market and does not pay income taxes. Investor-owned utilities have succeeded in effectively ending preference power and in obtaining significant tax subsidies that largely offset any tax advantage enjoyed by public power. They have also had great success in obtaining rates based on their version of the cost of service because of the inability of regulators to scrutinize their costs. The supposed competitive disadvantage of investor-owned utilities is an illusion.

There are two main reasons why public power produces comparable or better service at a lower cost. First, costs are likely to be kept lower when they are subject to political control. For example, pay increases for employees of the Los Angeles municipal electric utility are set by the City Council in open session. In sharp contrast, investor-owned utilities negotiate pay levels with employees without regulatory intervention. When pay levels are set in public view and by people who can be held responsible for their actions, the results are usually better for the consumer. The general manager in Los Angeles, heading a utility serving 1.5 million customers, is paid a fraction of what the CEO of a comparable investor-owned utility receives. As his utility provides rates 20 percent to 25 percent below those of neighboring power companies, there is no obvious reason that private sector executives should be paid more.

The second advantage is public power's nonprofit status. Investors need a return on equity, and the regulatory allowance for that amount is "grossed up" by regulators to allow the company enough money to pay taxes on the return before it gets paid to the investor. Because taxes are an allowable utility expense, consumers get to pay the taxes that protect the investors' return. Public power pays no return, meeting its capital requirements from borrowing and retained earnings. It borrows at tax-exempt rates, but even if it did not, it would retain much of its advantage by not collecting from its customers the high rates of return on equity and the taxes on them.

The case for public power is that it works. The case against it is that it works without making a profit. In campaigns against its introduction, investor-owned utilities question how anything run by government can work. They succeed in getting people to accept such doubts. The corporate use of massive amounts of money in campaigns against public power and the inability of the government to engage in campaign spending means that such untruths prevail.

Government cannot limit the First Amendment rights of power companies to campaign against public power. But it can adopt more positive and supportive policies to promote a system that is responsive to its customers and provides a service at low cost. Energy policy can cite public power as one method of lowering costs. A

single statement by a president or an act of Congress saying something favorable about the benefits of public power could have as
much effect on the market as thousands of adjustments by regulators. Federal and state governments could direct funds not to private developers but to public power to test and carry out
conservation and renewables programs; it would cost less and the
programs would be publicly accountable. Instead of treating public
power as a historical accident, more to be tolerated than emulated,
regulators could learn from public power's long experience as wires
companies purchasing some or all of their power supply from outside sources.

Perhaps the most significant restructuring that could occur in
the electric industry would be to allow customers as well as shareholders to participate in the decision to sell a utility. Small investor-
owned utilities are being acquired by larger companies, enhancing
the ability of the national power companies to dominate the
industry. When a utility is to be sold, its customers, whose interests
are usually entirely ignored, should be allowed to vote on a public-
power option. The shareholders of the selling company could be
protected by a mechanism that required the public entity to pay
either an amount equal to the best arm's-length offer or an amount
determined in a process similar to eminent-domain takings.

This process would increase the possibility that public power
could again be considered as a useful part of a newly restructured
industry. Conversion of small investor-owned utilities into public
power instead of favoring takeovers by ever-growing national
power companies would allow utilities to be more responsive to
their customers. Unfortunately, the rapid pace of utility mergers
leaves fewer and fewer opportunities for this proposal.

Utility rates could be made lower by the one element of public
policy—the support of public power—that is continually overlooked

because the power companies want no part of it. For government to claim to be looking out for the consumer without adopting policies to support and expand public power means that much electricity sector policy is a sham.

15. A better balance needs to be established between utility and consumer representation in regulatory proceedings

State consumer advocate offices need to be strengthened by better funding. A federal advocate should be created. Customers should no longer be required to pay the utilities' costs of litigating regulatory cases.

While almost all states have moved in recent years toward providing or allowing for regular representation of the consumer interest in utility regulatory matters, this has been more of a political gesture than one designed to produce significant results. Without adequate budgets, state consumer advocates cannot attain even the inadequate level of expertise of the regulators themselves. They are forced to react to utilities rather than being able to take the initiative. They are forced to measure their success by how much they have been able to cut from proposed rate increases. Even then, they do not have the resources to participate on anything like an equal footing with the utilities. Without increased funding, they will always risk being nothing more than window dressing.

One reasonable rule of thumb would be to require that the consumer advocate's budget be 50 percent of the regulatory commission's budget. Regulators do not represent consumers; they protect the public interest, including that of the power companies. Only if advocates get reasonable funding can consumers expect the same kind of aggressive participation in the regulatory process that the power companies exercise.

In most American civil legal proceedings, each party bears the responsibility of paying its own legal costs. This practice serves as something of a deterrent against bringing frivolous legal actions. However, in utility regulatory proceedings, the company is virtually assured that it can charge its regulatory costs as an operating expense to be recovered from customers. Such recovery is virtually automatic. As noted earlier, it usually results in the utilities' customers paying for both the company's costs and those of the consumer advocate, both of which are included in their rates. And they pay more for the utility's attempt to raise their rates than they do to defend their own interests.

Utilities have a fiduciary responsibility to their shareholders to maximize their profits. They have no legal obligation to customers to cut costs. Regulators only referee; they do not give first priority to protecting the consumer. It makes sense for the shareholders and the customers to cover their own costs; it does not make sense for the customers to pay for all costs—their own, the shareholders' and the regulators. The costs to utilities of participating in regulatory proceedings should be born solely by their shareholders. Aside from the justice inherent in this more balanced approach, the deterrent effect against starting proceedings should also benefit consumers.

The growth in FERC's role in making decisions that affect customer costs strongly suggests that the consumer needs direct representation before the federal regulatory body. The disappearance of the Oregon proposal to create a federal consumer advocate in the 2005 energy law that gave so much to the power companies—the repeal of PUHCA, the virtual elimination of PURPA power, tax breaks, native-load priority—is proof of the one-sidedness of the legislation. It would be a small but highly significant matter to provide some balance by creating the position of federal consumer advocate. The added costs would be tiny when compared with the unnecessary charges that have been imposed by ISOs.

The combination of these measures, coming at little or no added cost, would not guarantee any better results for customers. But they would level the playing field somewhat and create the opportunity for consumers—without giving them any special rights—to declare and defend their interests.

The electric utility industry imposes costs without commensurate benefit. It escapes careful scrutiny and uses the power of political contributions to gain an ever-increasing advantage over essentially helpless customers. Monopolies and oligopolies harm the economy when they extract excess revenues from their customers without a decent relationship to the underlying value of their service. It is harmful to the democratic system for government to aid exploitation by the power companies. The proposals made here do not roll back history, but they make possible the achievement of greater economic and political health in this vital sector of American life.

NOTES

1 This figure is derived by applying an overcharge of $0.005 or about 6.6 percent to each kilowatt-hour sold annually. This is a conservative number and includes excess profit from high returns on equity, from high rates set for competitive purposes and other sources described in the text, from the recovery from customers of utilities' regulatory costs, and from government surcharges.

2 The source of much of the Edison biographical material is Matthew Josephson, *Edison* (New York: McGraw-Hill, 1959).

3 The source of much of the Insull biographical material is Forest McDonald, *Insull* (Chicago: University of Chicago Press, 1962).

4 See IEEE Virtual Museum, "AC vs. DC: The Stuggle [sic] for Power," available at http://www.ieee-virtual-museum.org/collection/event.php?id= 3456872&lid=1.

5 Speech by Arthur Levitt reprinted in CFO, May 2003, available at http://www.cfo.com/article.cfm/3009202/c_3046591?f=magazine_featured.

6 McDonald, *op.cit.*, p. 333.

7 *Ibid.*

8 P.L. 74-333.

9 P.L. 73-17.

10 P.L. 75-329.

11 Ch. 687, Title II, 49 Stat. 838, August 26, 1935.

12 *Public Utilities Commission of Rhode Island v. Attleboro Steam and Electric Co.*, 273 U.S. 83 (1927).

13 P.L. 74-605.

14 P.L. 95-617.

15 Powerplant and Industrial Fuel Use Act, P.L. 95-620.

16 P.L. 95-619.

17 P.L. 95-617 through P.L. 95-621.

18 *Kansas City Power & Light Company v. State Corporation Commission*, 715 P.2d, 19, 479 U.S. 801 (1986). See also *FERC v. Mississippi*, 456 U.S. 742 (1982).

19 P.L. 102-486.

20 P.L. 75-688.

21 *New York v. FERC*, 535 U.S. 1 (2002).

22 National Grid quotes are from National Grid, "Transmission: The Critical Link," June 2005, available at http://www.nationalgridus.com/transmission/c3-3_documents.asp.

23 Office of U.S. Rep. Brian Baird, Press Release, December 13, 2002.

24 Devon Power LLC et al., FERC Docket No. ER03-563-030. Judge Bobbie J. McCartney, Initial Decision, June 15, 2005 at 105.

25 Both quotes are from Illinois Citizens Utility Board press release, Chicago, IL, October 18, 2005.

26 As quoted in Restructuring Today, August 30, 2005 (online subscription newsletter).

27 "The Deal That Even Awed Them in Houston," *The New York Times*, November 23, 2005 (online edition).

28 Alan R. Schriber, quoted in "Electric Dereg Termed Work in Progress," *Dayton Daily News*, August 9, 2005 (online edition).

29 Quoted in "Deregulation Falls Short of Promises," *Chicago Tribune*, October 23, 2005 (online edition).

30 Background information on Enron developments from Kurt Eichenwald, *Conspiracy of Fools* (New York: Broadway Books, 2005).

31 Ibid., p. 115.

32 Enron transcripts were obtained by the Snohomish County (Washington) Public Utility District (PUD). They were initially filed by Snohomish with FERC on May 17, 2004, and later supplemented. Transcript excerpts are posted on the Snohomish County PUD Web site (www.snopud.com) under

the title "Our Fight Against Enron." The Snohomish transcripts were the subject of Associated Press reports.

33 Report of Snohomish transcripts in Associated Press, "Utility: Enron Gouged Western Customers for at least $1.1 Billion, Manipulated Energy Market," June 14, 2004.

34 Ken Silverstein, "Enron Tapes Inflame Californians," *Issue Alert* (Utilipoint International), June 7, 2004 (online edition).

35 Eichenwald, op. cit., pp. 402–403.

36 *State of California v. FERC, U.S. Court of Appeals for the Ninth Circuit*, September 9, 2004.

37 Quoted in "The Blackout of 2003: The Context," *The New York Times*, August 15, 2005 (online edition).

38 Alex Radin, *Public Power—Private Life* (Washington, D.C.: American Public Power Association, 2003), p. 294. This book is the source of background on public power.

39 See U.S.-Canada Power System Outage Task Force, *Final Report on the August 14, 2003 Blackout in the United States and Canada: Causes and Recommendations* (April 2004). Online at: https://reports.energy.gov/.

40 U.S. House of Representatives, Committee on Energy and Commerce, release of MISO transcripts, September 3, 2003.

41 "Power Trader Tied to Bush Finds Washington All Ears," by Lowell Bergman and Jeff Gerth, *The New York Times*, May 25, 2001.

42 Rep. Billy Tauzin, chairman of the House Energy and Commerce Committee, Statement, August 15, 2003.

43 P.L. 109-058.

44 "Chicago-Based Utility's Parent Exelon Readies for Deregulated World," *Chicago Tribune*, June 4, 2004 (online edition).

45 Quoted in Power Marketing Association, *Daily Power Report* (online) from: *The Times*, Muncie, Indiana, April 15, 2005.,

46 Quoted in *Issue Alert* (UtiliPoint International), August 19, 2005 (online edition).

47 Quoted in Bruce W. Radford, "Electric Reliability Sanctions or Commerce?" *Public Utilities Fortnightly*, May 1, 1998 (Public Utilities Reports online: http://www.pur.com/pubs/2947.cfm).

48 "Benchmarking Air Emissions of the 100 Largest Electric Generation Owners in the United States—2000," Center for Environmentally Responsible Economics (CERES), Table ES-1, p. 5, online: http://www.ceres.org/pub/publication.php?pid=57; and U.S. Department of Energy, Energy Information Administration, "Net Generation By Energy Source by Type

of Producer," online: http://www.eia.doe.gov/cneaf/electricity/epa/
epat1p1.html.

49 "Duke Bites the Bullet on Wholesale Power," *Houston Chronicle*, September 14, 2005 (online edition).

50 "Mirant Deal a Tangled Web," *Atlanta Journal Constitution*, August 14, 2005 (online edition).

51 Quoted in "Westar Rate Proposals Would Challenge Utility's 'Survival,' " *Journal-World* (Lawrence, Kansas), October 5, 2005 (online edition).

52 Contribution data from www.opensecrets.org, based on filings with the Federal Election Commission. See http://www.opensecrets.org/industries/indus.asp?cycle=2006&ind=E08 and http://www.opensecrets.org/industries/contrib.asp?Ind=E08&Cycle=2002.

53 John Dunbar, "Nice Work If You Can Get It: Political Patronage Rules in State Utility Commissions," Center for Public Integrity, November 17, 2005, available at www.publicintegrity.orgtelecom/report.aspx?aid=762.

54 *Narragansett Electric Company v. Edward F. Burke*, 435 U.S. 972 (1978).

55 2005–06 Annual Directory & Statistical Report (Washington, D.C.: American Public Power Association, 2005), p. 28.

56 Radin, *op. cit.*, p. 139.

57 *Ibid.*, p. 212.

58 *Ibid.*, p. 229.

59 *Utah Power and Light Co. v. FERC*, 463 U.S. 1230 (1983)

60 *Clark-Cowlitz Joint Operating Agency v. FERC*, 826 F.2d. 1074 (1987).

61 *City of Colton v. Southern California Edison, FERC v. Southern California Edison*, 376 U.S. 205 (1964).

62 Ken Silverstein, "Electric Cooperatives on the Move," *Issue Alert* (UtiliPoint International), June 2, 2004 (online edition).

63 *Ibid.*

64 See http://www.opensecrets.org/industries/contrib.asp?Ind=E08&Cycle=2004

65 Statement by Glenn English, CEO, NRECA, July 29, 2005, online at: http://www.nreca.coop/Documents/PublicPolicy/20050729.pdf.

66 Calculated from statistical data from the National Association of State Utility Consumer Advocates provided to author.

INDEX